An American Homeplace

BOOKS BY DONALD McCAIG

Novels

The Butte Polka
Nop's Trials

Entertainments

Stalking Blind
The Man Who Made the Devil Glad
The Bamboo Cannon

Nonfiction

Eminent Dogs, Dangerous Men

Poetry

Last Poems

An American Homeplace
Donald McCaig

CROWN PUBLISHERS, INC.
NEW YORK

Published by Crown Publishers, Inc., 201 East 50th Street, New York,
New York 10022. Member of the Crown Publishing Group.

CROWN is a trademark of Crown Publishers, Inc.

Manufactured in the United States of America

Book design by Linda Kocur

Library of Congress Cataloging-in-Publication Data

McCaig, Donald.
An American homeplace/by Donald McCaig.
1. McCaig, Donald—Homes and haunts—Virginia.   2. Novelists, American
—20th century—Biography.   3. Highland County (Va.)—Social life and
customs.   4. Farm life—Virginia—Highland County.   5. Sheep ranchers—
Virginia—Biography.   6. Highland County (Va.)—History.   I. Title.
PS3563.A2555Z463   1992
813'.54—dc20

[B]   91-43101
                                                                          CIP

ISBN 0-517-58487-5

10   9   8   7   6   5   4   3   2   1

First Edition

FOR KNOX BURGER—LITERARY GENTLEMAN

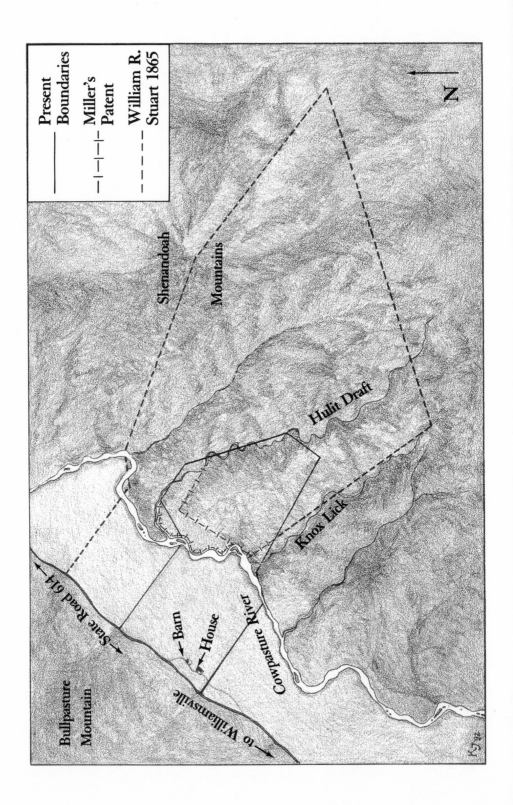

Contents

Contents

PART I

An American Homeplace

During the Summer of Love, 1969, Anne and I lived on St. Mark's Place in the East Village. We were right around the corner from the Fillmore East, where Janis Joplin and Otis Redding and the Who and the Doors played Rock & Roll. By day, I was the copy chief of a hot advertising agency. By night, I was Snee the poet. I kept my worlds completely distinct. Downtown, my friends didn't know what I did for a living. I never saw my uptown colleagues after five. Though this behavior probably wasn't sane, in those days it wasn't unusual. My friends were Billy Budd and Mark, Long John and Sheena, Simon, the Custer brothers, Cousins, Spanky, Pooh-dog, and Pearl of the North Woods. Some of my friends, I never did learn their Christian names. It would have been rude to ask. It was rude to ask about families or where you worked. "What do you do?" was a tourist's question.

*   *   *

34 St. Mark's Place, where Anne and I had an apartment, was across the street from what had been the Dom, the Ukrainian Social Hall, now painted blue and renamed The Electric Circus. Weekend mornings early, I'd pick my way down our stoop through the runaways sleeping there. Day-Glo sparkles, painted faces, wilted flowers — they were flotsam from the street carnival of the night before. At intervals, the Ukrainian chiropractor on the first floor would scurry out and curse and sluice buckets of water down the stoop. These kids were ruining his livelihood. His customers were elderly and frail and afraid to pass through these stoned, inexplicable children.

Nowadays, deep in the country, I'm a citizen. I vote, work the precinct, teach a class at the community college. Every year I bake a couple loaves of bread for the Presbyterian ladies' lawn party. I was born to be a lawn party baker.

In 1968, I joined SDS. That was a time when murderers were abroad in the land. Men who spoke up—Robert Kennedy, Martin Luther King, Fred Hampton—were routinely murdered. Souls in the basement of the zeitgeist pulled the triggers—there was no paper trail connecting Sirhan Sirhan to the powers that be, but everybody understood the message: Get out far in front and you'll get shot; run in the front ranks and you're in for all the trouble the culture can dish out.

My SDS group was loosely attached to the New School, and most members were sons and daughters of traditional New York lefties. They used phrases like "Imperialist Powers" and "Running Dog Lackeys" like those odd words meant something. Their anger was in the right place, but it was hard to stay awake through the meetings, which never broke up until two or three in the morning. We met on Avenue D.

Part of the New York hippie uniform was a Buck knife, a folding hunter, which rode in a closed holster on the belt. I suppose the knife symbolized a sort of loft-carpenter industry, a no-nonsense down-hominess. After SDS meetings I'd go home through the meanest part of the city, walking right down the middle of the street, past burned-out tenements, wheelless stripped cars, one hand on my knife, afraid.

Some of my SDS friends ended up pictured on post office walls. It was a sick feeling to see people I'd liked, who I mostly agreed with, in such desperate trouble.

Demonstration mornings, Anne and I would assemble with all the others at five o'clock in Union Square. We drank coffee from paper cups as we filed onto the waiting buses. I don't know where they found those buses, but by the time we hit the Maryland Turnpike, every rattletrap, smoke-belching, antique charter bus in New England was en route to D.C., nose to tail in a column that stretched for miles.

The sun hung in a steamy ball over Maryland's foggy green grass while terribly earnest teenage MOBE marshals advised us about tear gas: Cover your face with Vaseline, clap wet handkerchiefs over your mouths, don't rub your eyes.

Friends had rented a big country house in New Hampshire, and twenty of us came together that Thanksgiving to wander their snowy woods, play music, fetch pitchers of hard cider from the barrel in the cellar. Several skidded their cars into the ditch, a dog bit a kid, and I wondered how in the world they'd last until spring with the puny stack of firewood on their porch. When we got home to New York, junkies had tried to crowbar the door of our apartment, but the door proved too stout for them.

My advertising accounts included Renault, After Six Tuxedoes, Dubonnet wine, Club Mediteranée, and Georg Jensen. In 1968, I won the New York Advertising Club's silver medal for my

Georg Jensen campaign. Since I wasn't at the awards banquet, they mailed the medal to me, encased in plastic. I forwarded it to my parents, who hoped it augured well for my future.

On Wednesday, Thursday, and Sunday nights, after eleven, I'd stop in Googie's Bar, on Thompson Street. Draft beer was sixty cents and the only imported beer, Heineken, was a buck. In saloon society, I knew two cats and one dog named Heineken.

The bartender, Lorenzo Boelitz, bought a hundred acres of land in northern Maine, a few miles shy of the Canadian border. The land was cut over second growth, rock maple and spruce that fronted the Moose River. Lorenzo invited his bar pals to come north and help him build a log cabin.

I suppose thirty people worked on that cabin, off and on, during that light-struck summer. Perhaps four had ever used a hammer before.

We shouldered brutally heavy peeled logs and stumbled through the tuckerbrush because nobody knew how to skid them. Afraid of the nasty-looking adz, we fashioned elaborate shin guards of twelve-inch spikes lashed with cord. Since there was no road into the property, we floated the flooring lumber down the river from the town of Jackman, our raft ballasted with cases of cold beer.

Because I was an ex-Marine, I was in charge of sanitation; I dug the pit privy and kept it limed and covered. I should have paid attention to the river water too, which we all drank and which produced dysentery and some Owsley-grade hallucinations.

We were sitting around the campfire one night, passing joints around, listening to Woody Guthrie tunes chasing the embers into the night, where both became stars.

Looking around my circle of friends, I really did think things could change, we could really save the world; if only we could act together, no force on earth could resist us.

"Three," I announced solemnly, "is better than two."

Spanky broke a guitar string, sighed, and laid his Martin against a stump. There was this moment as my wisdom settled into everyone's stoned being. The stars swirled overhead. Somewhere downstream a loon cried its haunting cry.

"Except snakebites," Spanky amended.

We swam in the river every afternoon, but our blue jeans were pungent with wood smoke and Cutter's fly dope. One afternoon we canoed into town for supplies and I was admiring the red-and-black wool shirts in Armand Pomerlau's general store when Armand came over. "Any of you fellows named Donald McCaig? If he's here, his office called."

My account exec said the Renault account was in trouble. Renault was the agency's biggest account, a quarter of our billing, and the client wanted a brand-new television campaign. Sure, the AE knew I'd planned to stay away another month, but I'd been gone for five weeks already. . . .

Standing outdoors at the pay phone, watching the Moose River flow under the bridge, our canoes bobbing in the sparkling water, I said, "No. Give the account to somebody else. I'll be back in the fall."

I do remember how galled I felt. My two realities, two names, had collided with a bang. I didn't want to be a person with an office and didn't want them phoning me here. It would be years before I understood what decision I'd made there on that riverbank: that I would never be a vice president, that I was that smelly unshaven river rat, not the smooth-talking copywriter with a different name.

That was the happiest time of my life and I knew it wouldn't last, that things were bound to get worse for me. Since blindness is the guide dog of unhappiness, I made my decisions quick while I could see. I'd marry Anne, if she'd have me. I'd get some friends together and go to the country.

* * *

I was born in a mining town in Montana. When I came to New York City, I expected the city to change me. That's why the young people come—to be someone different, to understand the ways of power, to learn what we'd been protected from. The first night I was in the city, I walked down Waverly Place thinking how many people had died here, in this city, how their souls had adhered to the facades of the brick loft buildings, the gilded windows offering HATS, FINE MEN'S HATS, the black, greasy cobblestones.

Four hundred and fifty million years ago, our farm lay at the bottom of a shallow sea that extended from the Gulf of Mexico to Newfoundland. As the earth rose and fell, tilted and eroded, the sea drained off, mountains lunged, eroded again, and the sea came back. Parts of Highland County, Virginia, where we're located, have been under sea three times. Each time, the rivers peeled the mountains back, depositing silt, marine and vegetable fossils. During fortunate times, life was plentiful in a warm sea; during other periods, erosion was so swift, foul water choked most life out.

Geologists call this the Valley and Ridge Province: long linear valleys and softened old mountains traveling south by west, bounded by the Allegheny Front and the Shenandoah Valley. The pattern of uplands and dips is regular and resembles the fossilized wave patterns we sometimes find on the limestone rocks, as if the region has provided its own maps.

Our farm lies in the upper Cowpasture River Valley between the Bullpasture and Shenandoah mountains. Bullpasture Mountain is a steep syncline of limestone shale and sandstone. A cutaway diagram is provided 12 miles north where U.S. 250 cuts through the mountain. From bottom to top are 1,000 feet of Millboro shale, 150 feet of Onondaga shale, 200 feet of fossiliferous Oriskany sandstone, 775 of Helderberg limestone, and 595 feet of Keyser limestone. The limestone bands were the reefs of that ancient sea, and the sandstone was the beaches.

8

Across our river is Shenandoah Mountain, a thirty-mile-long anticline, with its shale layers closer to the surface. Ridges and hollows and peaks, Shenandoah Mountain is gentler than Bullpasture Mountain, but higher too: 3,975 feet at Wallace Peak.

Shenandoah Mountain is part of the George Washington National Forest, so nobody lives there. Most of Bullpasture Mountain is State Game Commission land, and nobody lives there either.

In the spring of 1716, rangers (frontier scouts) informed Virginia's Governor Spotswood of a pass they'd found in the Blue Ridge. Although it was thought that lands west of the Blue Ridge were infertile and populated by fierce Indians, Governor Spotswood proposed an expedition. The governor wasn't attracted to these lands, he was pushed.

In 1618, Virginia and Maryland's combined tobacco exports totaled twenty thousand pounds; in 1627, half a million pounds; in 1709, nearly thirty million. The planters who settled Virginia looked to England for their values, aspirations, and markets. Tobacco fetched a good price, it didn't weigh much, and it could be shipped all the way across the Atlantic. The Tidewater planters embraced the crop eagerly.

Tobacco was a labor-intensive crop that required much hand labor, and most of those hands were black. It was commonly calculated that tobacco plantations of less than a thousand acres were unprofitable and each fifty acres required one slave. The accepted crop rotation was: year one, tobacco; year two, tobacco; year three, tobacco; year four, wheat; years five and six, corn; year seven, gullies.

The great plantations crept across the Tidewater like tremendous slugs, ingesting thousands of acres of fertile virgin soil and leaving desert behind. In the winter the slaves felled the forest where Year One Tobacco would be planted next spring.

The plantation's best land was reserved for tobacco, as was the attention of the total work force. Few plantations grew productive gardens. During summer months scrawny cattle and hogs roamed the untillable swamps. Like modern Midwestern farmers, the plantations bought most of their food supply.

Farming such vast properties (and English land-use traditions) created a new job: overseer. Since the overseer was paid a simple percentage of the crops he raised, maximum short-term production was his only goal. Hang the land. Hang the slaves.

By 1700, tobacco planters were producing more tobacco in two years than all Europe could smoke in three. The plantations had grown enormous—some were a hundred thousand acres—and they drove the smaller farmers out. Small farmers and the tobacco planters alike cried for virgin land west of the Blue Ridge.

A 1711 petition from the Maryland Council to the king describes "the miserable and deplorable circumstances of many good planters, to whom their serv'ts. and slaves are become even burthensome by the low price of tobaccos at home. The generallity of the Planters, especially such as have shipped their tobaccos to their correspondents in London, are become greatly indebted to the merchants and very many of their plantations and stocks are wholy mortgaged and forefyed to them, and others dayly desert their abodes for feare of being imprisoned. . . ."

When Spotswood's expedition assembled in the fall of 1716, a dozen Virginia Gentlemen were accompanied by twice their number of rangers and Indian scouts. They followed the Rappahanock River to its source, high in the Blue Ridge Mountains. One gentleman got into a hornets' nest and swelled up dreadfully. Fevers discommoded others. The diarist, John Fontaine, wrote that they "made great fires and supped and drank good punch. By ten of the clock I had taken all of my ounce of Jesuit's Bark, but my head was much out of order."

They shot three bear and a giant rattlesnake. When Fontaine shot a deer from his horse, the horse bucked him off and ran away. Several men fell sick with measles and were left behind in a sick camp. On the fifth of September, they achieved the summit of the Blue Ridge at Swift Run Pass, where they drank to King George's health. Fontaine went off to sightsee and lost his gun. On the sixth, using a trail blazed by Indians, they descended into the Shenandoah Valley and made camp beside the Shenandoah River. There they "drank the King's health in champagne, and fired a volley, the Princess's health in Burgundy and fired a volley, and all the rest of the Royal Family in claret, and a volley. We drank the Governor's health and fired another volley. We had several sorts of liquors, viz, Virginia red wine and white wine, Irish usquebaugh (whiskey), brandy, shrub, two sorts of champagne, canary, cherry, punch, water, cider, &c."

The Spotswood Expedition was a Colonial version of Woodstock.

It is tempting to cast tobacco as the sole villain of Colonial agriculture, but the planters didn't need tobacco to fail. Even mediocre virgin soil was fertile for a few years, and land was so inexpensive (less than a penny an acre) that Thomas Jefferson claimed that it was cheaper to clear new soil than conserve the old. Of course, Thomas Jefferson is a famous agricultural bankrupt. George Washington only kept Mount Vernon from the same fate by the sale of western lands.

Agriculture, as Wendell Berry reminds us, is first "culture," and planter agricultural culture proved ruinous. These men grew for a distant cash market, they owned tremendous means of production (slaves), which became the tail that wagged the dog (one Virginia planter told of growing tobacco even when he lost money because otherwise he'd have no winter work—clearing—for his slaves to do).

They were "Virginia Gentlemen," "English Country Squires transplanted to a warm climate and turned slave-masters"—that's how Francis Parkman, the great American historian, described them. Their self-creation included many first-rate horsemen, dozens of fourth-rate poets, a few inventors, plenty of brilliant generals, some spectacular drunks, and orators we still quote today.

But more hurtful to the land than tobacco, overseers, market agriculture, even the cavalier aristocracy, was one simple fact: These men did not understand Virginia soils.

Unfortunately, opening the lands beyond the Blue Ridge didn't relieve pressure on Tidewater soils. The western lands that Spotswood spied, rolling endlessly beyond the Shenandoah Valley, were not settled by planters and never grew much tobacco. A different sort of farmer settled beyond the Blue Ridge.

In the 1700s, waves of immigrant Germans and Scotch Irish arrived in Pennsylvania because Pennsylvania, of all the colonies, promised the greatest religious freedom. As it happened, many of these new immigrants landed at the Colony of New Sweden on Delaware Bay, where Celtic newcomers learned how to build log house and fences of rails.

Rather than intermingling as they came up the great Valley, the Scotch-Irish and Germans tumbled over each other, founding a Scotch-Irish settlement here (Presbyterian), a German there (Brethren, Mennonite). The Scotch-Irish had been livestock men in Ulster, herders, and the Germans were tillage farmers. At the time, the Scotch-Irish were viewed as (a) fierce, (b) courageous, (c) hard drinking, (d) hardy prayers, (e) respecters of learning, (f) good Indian fighters, (g) poor farmers. The Germans were supposed to be pacific and better farmers.

The settling of the frontier is one of America's core myths. Two hundred fifty years afterward, during the summer months in our mountains, groups of enthusiasts (buckskinners) rendezvous to reenact their fantasies of the American frontier. They shoot black-powder guns, throw knives, hurl tomahawks, drink to excess. Wearing handmade garments and abjuring all artifacts post-1834, they live out a dream of frontier anarchy when men were men and women had babies — when any man bold enough to cut a farm out of the wilderness and hold it against pesky redskins could advance himself and his family.

But this is a very modern picture. 1745 when Augusta County, Virginia, was formed, was thirty years prior to the Declaration of Independence with its radical vision of equality. Though John Locke's ideas were familiar to men of Jefferson and Washington's class, it would be years before they'd trickle into ordinary understanding. In 1745, presented with the notion "All men are created equal," most frontiersmen would have believed that a condition to be remedied, not a state to be admired.

Settlers rolled south down the Shenandoah Valley into Augusta County and slipped west through the gaps into the narrower valleys: the Calfpasture River Valley, the Cowpasture, the Bullpasture, and the Jackson.

Rangers explored the upper Cowpasture River Valley in 1721 and there were settlers here by 1740, William and Jane Stuart and Patrick Miller among them. The upper Cowpasture runs from the forks at Shaw's Ridge to Williamsville, two miles below our farm, where the Bullpasture joins the Cowpasture.

The valley is almost the size of Manhattan Island and presently has twenty-eight inhabitants, five of them children. The unpaved state road winds along the river, crossing at Shaw's Fork and again at Laurel Gap. The few bad roads that climb into the flanking mountains are infrequently used by loggers, hunters, and ginseng root gatherers. At its broadest points, the river-bottom land is a half mile wide. The river is choked down by cliffs at Benson's Run and Laurel Gap.

It is a remote, wild, and lonely valley today.

Sixty acres of our farm is farmable. The house and outbuildings are set in an alluvial fan at the base of Bullpasture Mountain, and the state road traverses that mountain a hundred yards above the steading. The river runs on the far side of our flat land, tucked up against the shale cliffs of Shenandoah Mountain. Above those cliffs, ridges rise in gentle undulations, one after another, crossed only by a nineteenth-century footpath, the Jerkemtight Trail and

Sugar Tree Road, a logging road, which flanks the mountain, far above our land.

Our mountain land, ninety acres on Shenandoah Mountain, is mostly wooded. This is Southern hardwood forest: red oak, black oak, crimson oak, white oak, pin oak, red, sugar, and rock maple, tulip poplar, wild cherry, yellow birch, sycamore, locust, black walnut, hickory, some hemlock, white pine, and cedar. Cedar is reclaiming the narrow field across the river, and the half-acre pastures beside the woods road that climbs into the mountain are hard to distinguish today.

Since the farm lies at nineteen hundred feet above sea level, we are the southernmost tip of a climate zone that stretches northward into coastal Maine. Although winter temperatures can drop to twenty below, our growing season is fairly long (May 16 and October 1 are typical frost dates). Snow rarely stays on the ground longer than three weeks, and it is not unusual to have a period of shirt-sleeve weather in January. In normal years, our sheep graze on stockpiled grass until Thanksgiving and we stop feeding hay on IRS day.

Summers are cool; temperatures that hit ninety are uncharacteristic, and we need neither fans nor air conditioners at night. Our worst weather is March winds, which can gust up to sixty or eighty mph and can pluck the roof off a house or barn. Although our steading lies between two long finger slopes snugged against the Bullpasture, there've been cold spring nights when our log house rocked and groaned like a ship breasting a hurricane.

We get forty inches of rainfall annually. June rains come down the valley like clockwork, between four and five every afternoon. Our snowstorms come the same way, west to east, concealing the mountaintop, then the ridges, then the tree fringe on the edge of the river, ladylike as lace curtains fluttering in the wind.

The first settlers entered the Cowpasture Valley fifteen miles to the south through Panther Gap, where a rough wagon road terminated at Green Valley Farm. They'd traveled two days from Staunton (at the time known as Beverley's Mill Place). Green Valley was half farm, half fort, with a blockhouse to resist attack by the Indians. From Green Valley, the settlers traveled northwest up a narrow trail (pack horses only) along Indian Draft. They forded the river back and forth. Near the junction where Williamsville would be built, they'd ford three times in a mile. The river-bottom land was a brushy, tangled floodplain, wetlands here and there. The mountainsides were climax forest, great leafy spaces under a high canopy overhead. Deer would bound away from their passage. A bison would lift its placid head from its grazing.

Along the trail they passed small log cabins, windowless, dirt floored, not very different from the hog houses that were the only outbuildings. Finally, where the track narrowed and quit, they'd reach the branch that marked the start of *their* land. Perhaps before dark their guide would walk the perimeter with them. That night, they'd lie by the fire listening to the wolves howl on the mountainside.

In those days Augusta County *was* the western frontier and stretched from the Shenandoah Valley of Virginia north to Pittsburgh, including most of what is presently West Virginia to the Ohio River in the west.

Picture yourself, a young immigrant just arrived at Beverley's Mill Place, your wife and wee bairn in tow. Outside the new county courthouse (who would have thought there'd be such a furious bustle of comings and goings here on the frontier?), you accost a man who looks prosperous, a man of consequence.

"Pardon me, sir ..." You explain that you wish to settle on a piece of land, nothing grand, mind. Just enough so a growing family can make a living.

"Very well. Beverley has land for sale. Borden and Lewis too."

"Sir, I was thinking about maybe patenting land myself. In one of yon mountain valleys. I herded stock in the mountains, you see, sir, and have a special fondness for them."

Your adviser says that first you must locate the land you want, then apply for a warrant from the Council in Williamsburg.

"Fine, then," you grin. "I'll be applying for Ohio."

Your adviser is not amused. "You won't get a deed for any large tract until you can prove you have settled one family per thousand acres. Can you manage that?"

Your wife tugs your sleeve. Your sense of humor has got you in difficulties before. "Just two hundred acres," you say. "Well watered, a bit of bottom land. Well timbered. Fertile."

"First you find your land, then you have Thomas Lewis survey it—"

"He'll be the same Lewis you mentioned, the fellow what's selling his own land?"

"The same. Mr. Lewis is a very busy man. And if he finds time to do your survey, he'll post it here at the courthouse, and if there's no objection, after a year, you apply for a patent."

"And if there's an objection . . ."

"You can't go out there and settle on another's land. It's not a wilderness, you know."

"And how will I know that the land I discover isn't already claimed by another?"

"I'm sure I don't know." And the man hurries away.

Your wife tells you it's September, which you bloody well know, and that you'll be wanting some shelter for the winter. Beyond the muddy streets of Beverley's Mill Place, the mountains stretch out in ranks, blue tinged, row on row.

Early on, men like Lewis and Borden and Beverley took up tremendous grants—Lewis had thirty thousand acres on the Cow-pasture alone—and these men did want settlers on that land to satisfy the Council's one-settler-per-thousand-acres requirement. So you go to Lewis and offer to pay him in three years for a

16

hundred sixty acres on his Cowpasture River land. You'll bring deer and bear hides into Beverley's Mill Place, wolf heads for the three-shilling bounty. (In 1745, three hundred wolf heads were brought to the Augusta County Courthouse.) Perhaps you shake hands with Mr. Lewis and the great man introduces you to the ranger who'll guide you to your property. You'll have signed a paper promising not to sell your land until a year after you get your deed, you'll have posted a bond to guarantee your word.

Two or three years later, after seasons of terrific work and near starvation (the baby almost certainly will have died), you pay Mr. Lewis's agent the sum agreed upon and ask for your deed.

Mr. Lewis is in the Colonial capital Williamsburg, or the original survey has been disputed or he can't give you your deed until he's finished settling the tract or . . . or . . .

Although the large freeholders received title to their tracts as soon as they proved that land was settled, there was no legal requirement that title be transferred to the settlers, and where the original freeholders could avoid deeding land, they did so. The batting average for actually getting your deed was less than fifty percent. Often the immigrant found himself in possession of a farm he was improving for the great owner, without a deed or the option of selling portions of it to more recent arrivals.

The big freeholders thought land was too important to give to poor immigrants; in 1745 more than two-thirds of the white males in Augusta County didn't own an inch of it. In that same year, John Lewis and his son Thomas were involved in three-quarters of the sales of land to new landowners.

If, like William Stuart, you were a schoolteacher, not a herds-man—if you could sit down with John Lewis and speak his language, well then, a way might be found. Or suppose you were Patrick Miller, son of freeholder John Miller, who'd been a Lewis associate for years. . . . "Patrick, there's a nice piece on the Cow-pasture, some good fields under the Shenandoah Mountain. . . ." One of us. One of us.

*   *   *

Our farmable land is a half-mile strip between Bullpasture Mountain and the Cowpasture River. River and mountain created this land and limit our farming practices today. Our big floods come in the fall, when the ground is already saturated and hurricanes or tropical storms stall over the mountains. In 1710, the James River, which is fed by the Cowpasture, crested at Richmond forty feet above flood tide. In this century we've had what state officials (with laudable modesty) call "two-hundred-year floods" in 1913, 1926, 1949, 1973, and 1985.

After the floodwaters squeeze through Laurel Gap, they fan out onto our fields, to deposit their loads of silt and gravel. Since the current is strongest near the river, that's where the bigger rocks drop. Away from the river, floodwaters deposit finer silt. Though soil scientists have identified ten distinct soil types on this farm, it is helpful to think of three soil bands: riverside, valley bottom, and (Bullpasture) mountainside. Riverside is five to eight hundred yards of chagrin silt loam: rocky, good drainage, productive, and prone to periodic flooding.

That narrow overgrown field across the river, where Patrick Miller first settled in 1750, is chagrin. He built his one-room cabin on a low rise overlooking the field, well above floodwaters.

Valley bottom is Purdy silt loam, a thin layer of topsoil covering six to eight feet of white clay. In these flat fields, water stands on top of the soil until it evaporates. This soil is greasy, acid, sour on the tongue.

Where the Bullpasture Mountain starts to rise is a narrow band of Cataco loam: deep, fertile, and self-liming. From the cant of our fence and barn posts, I'd estimate this soil is flowing downslope an eighth to a quarter inch every year.

Our frost line is eighteen inches.

Since limestone is water soluble, the substrate here is honeycombed with caves and sinkholes and limestone conduits through which underground streams make their way. Since the sandstone is impermeable to water, sandstone layers provide floors for our water tables.

Two hundred-fifty years after Patrick Miller first settled here, his footprints are almost gone. Although there was a collapsed chimney at Miller's cabin site within living memory, there's nothing there now.

Miller's homeplace: fields, outbuildings, and house, formed a seventeen-acre triangle bounded by the river. Miller was a forest farmer, girdling the trees so they'd shed their leaves and his livestock could graze on the grass that came into the sunlight.

The Scotch-Irish settled on streamsides to avoid the necessity of digging a well. They farmed the woods instead of the easier river fields because they believed these floodplains were infertile. After their experience in Ireland, they called ground that didn't grow trees "barrens."

Miller ate bear and deer, possum and coon. His first crop was Indian corn, grown in hills with pumpkins surrounding each hill and beans climbing the stalks. Most of his sheep were killed by bears and wolves, but his hogs thrived in the woods. Hog meat was the meat of choice because if cured, it would keep. Sheep were kept for wool, cows for milk, butter, cheese, and market. Patrick Miller would have sold bear, beaver, fox, and wolf hides. He may have sold ginseng, too. He would have striven to be self-sufficient, to create an intelligent farm.

If Patrick Miller ever married, his wife died young—there is no mention of her nor her dower rights in Miller's deeds. Robert Miller settled downriver, on both sides, and presumably the brothers farmed together.

It was a grand time on the Cowpasture. Settlers were trickling in; early arrivals were speculating in land. Patents that they'd got for a penny an acre, they sold for a pound. By 1749, settlers had built a church on Pheasanty Run, south of Williamsville. It was only a log hut, but it was a *Presbyterian* log hut. They could worship as they liked, but only Anglican clergy could perform the most important ceremonies and until 1785, settlers would travel back into Staunton to get married. A Mr. Feamster, who was instrumental in building that first church, also built a blockhouse on pilings over a pond. A few souls snickered at him—the Indians were peaceful.

In 1757, the French built a substantial log fort, Fort Duquesne, at the junction of the Monongahela and Ohio rivers, where Pittsburgh stands today. Virginia's Colonial Governor Dinwiddie sent a young Lieutenant George Washington to the fort to object. Washington was received haughtily and had great trouble keeping his Indian rangers from deserting to the French, who had already enlisted the Shawnee, Delaware, Wyandott, and Miami.

Although formally at peace with France, the British decided to launch a series of preemptive (surgical?) strikes at French interests. General Braddock, with two regiments of British regulars, was ordered to attack Fort Duquesne.

These regiments, accompanied by Virginians under Washington's command, axed a twelve-foot road through the virgin forest. They moved about three miles a day. Two months after he entered the wilderness, Braddock's command approached Fort Duquesne, where they were ambushed by the French and Indians, who made a meal of them. The Indians crouched down behind trees, firing, whooping, while the redcoats fired militarily correct ineffectual volleys into the smoke. When the Virginians adopted those tactics, Braddock furiously shouted them back into order.

Later that evening Braddock remarked, "Who would have thought it?" and died.

James Smith, an American prisoner at Fort Duquesne, reported on the aftermath of the battle:

> In the afternoon I again observed a great noise and commotion in the fort, and, though at that time I could not understand French, I found it was the voice of joy and triumph, and feared that they had received what I called bad news. I had observed some of the old-country soldiers speak Dutch;

as I spoke Dutch, I went to one of them and asked him what was the news. He told me that a runner had just arrived who said that Braddock would certainly be defeated; that the Indians and French had surrounded him, and were concealed behind trees and in gullies, and kept a constant fire upon the English; and that they saw the English falling in heaps; and if they did not take the river, which was the only gap, and make their escape, there would not be one man left alive before sundown. Some time after this, I heard a number of scalp-halloos, and saw a company of Indians and French coming in. I observed they had a great number of bloody scalps, grenadiers' caps, British canteens, bayonets, etc., with them. They brought the news that Braddock was defeated. After that another company came in, which appeared to be about one hundred, and chiefly Indians; and it seemed to me that almost every one of this company was carrying scalps. After this came another company with a number of wagon-horses, and also a great many scalps. Those that were coming in and those that had arrived kept a constant firing of small arms, and also the great guns in the fort, which were accompanied with the most hideous shouts and yells from all quarters, so that it appeared to me as though the infernal regions had broke loose.

About sundown I beheld a small party coming in with a dozen prisoners, stripped naked, with their hands tied behind their backs and their faces and parts of their bodies blackened; these prisoners they burned to death on the bank of the Alleghany River, opposite the fort. I stood on the fort wall until I beheld them begin to burn one of these men; they had him tied to a stake, and kept touching him with firebrands, red-hot irons, etc., and he screaming in a most doleful manner, the Indians in the meantime yelling like infernal spirits. As this scene appeared too shocking for me to behold, I retired to my lodging both sore and sorry.

Braddock's defeat so terrified the British that they withdrew across the mountains, up the valley to Winchester, and thinking that might not be far enough, they retired to Philadelphia, leaving the frontier unprotected. Indians jogged down the nice road Braddock had made for them. They killed dozens on the Cowpasture. In his journal, Hugh McAden wrote, "A cold shuddering possessed every breast, and paleness covered almost every face. In short, the whole inhabitants were put into universal confusion. Scarcely any man durst sleep in his own house—but all met in companies with their wives and children, and set about building little fortifications to defend themselves. . . ."

Roads returning to Shenandoah Valley from the west were choked with refugees. Cabins were burned, crops abandoned.

The Cowpasture Valley served as the military anchor of Virginia's western frontier. George Washington ordered forts to be built: Fort George, Fort Lewis, Fort Nelson (Green Valley Farm), Fort Dickerson. Located on the great landowners' farms, manned by a handful of regulars, these forts were refuges for the settlers who were warned by patrolling rangers when Indian raiding parties came into the valley.

> According to Wilson family legend: John [Wilson] had gone to Dickinson's Fort, not far away, to get some help for the house-raising next day; while William, Jr. (called Thomas by others), had gone to a little mill, about a mile distant, to get some meal ground for the house-raising party.
>
> Two of the sisters, Margaret and Elizabeth, were out on the river bank washing flax-tow; Mrs. Wilson, who was in feeble health, had walked out where they were at work; an Irishman had a loom in the yard and was weaving; two of the sisters, Susan and Barbara, were in the cabin ironing the family clothes, and the father, with some other men, were at work on the new house logs, when the attack was made.
>
> In returning from the Fort, John encountered the Indians suddenly, in a turn of the road. They fired on him, and a ball passed through his clothes just under his arm, cutting the gusset of his shirt. He wheeled his horse quickly and fled back to the Fort to get immediate help to go to the rescue of the family, and about twenty returned with him.
>
> The Indians had passed on to the cabin. The girls at the river washing saw them coming and started to run, and at the same time tried to help their mother away, but she told them to go and save themselves and leave her. In passing, an Indian threw a tomahawk at the old lady, and severely wounded her in the wrist as she threw up her hand to save

her face. The Indians did not pursue them, but hurried on to the cabin. They fired at the Irish weaver, but he escaped with a flesh wound in his shoulder.

As they entered the cabin, one of the girls, Barbara, ran out and was knocked down and her skull probably fractured, but she was not scalped. The girl remaining in the cabin, Susan, closed the door, and when an Indian put his hand in to try to open it, she mashed and burned his fingers with a hot smoothing iron.

By this time, the father and his men from the new house foundation came up, and attacked the Indians with hand-spikes and foot-adze; the latter, in the hands of Mr. Wilson, and drove them off.

When John and his party arrived it was dark, and they were unable to see what mischief had been done. They ascended an elevated point near by, to see if they could discover any fire-light or other evidences of life about the cabin.

Seeing none, they concluded or feared that the family had all been destroyed. In nearing the cabin other dangers suggested themselves; the family had several fierce dogs, which had been trained to great watchfulness, some were taught to sleep at the back door of the cabin, and some at the front, so as to give warning of approaches from either direction; it also occurred to them that if any of the family survived, they would have sentries stationed to watch for a possible return of the Indians during the night, and that these sentries might fire on them. In the uncertainties, John Wilson himself took the lead, cautiously approached the cabin, and succeeded in reaching it without accident or alarm.

Upon entering the cabin he was rejoiced to find his father and sister Susan present and unharmed, but was at the same time pained to find his sister Barbara badly wounded, and his mother, two sisters, his brother William and the Irish weaver all missing, and their fates unknown.

At early dawn next morning, John and his party started out to search for the missing ones. He tracked his mother by her blood about a mile up the river, to where she had alternately walked and crawled, probably not knowing whither she went. When found she was entirely out of her mind and did not recognize her son and friends, supposing them to be Indians still pursuing her; she rallied however, and lived for many years afterward.

William, Jr., though he usually wore moccasins, had on the day before put on a pair of shoes. Going toward the mill the searchers found by his shoe tracks where he had attempted to run when the Indians discovered him—where he had slipped and fallen and been captured by them—where, further along, they had tied him to a tree, and afterwards loosened him again, and taken him off with them. His father always thought that if he had had on moccasins instead of shoes he would have escaped and avoided capture. His pursuers were confident that he had made his shoe-track 'sign' as conspicuous as possible, so as to enable them to follow the trail, but they never overtook him, and he was carried off to the Indian towns beyond the Ohio.

A returned prisoner reported to the family, some time after, that she had seen him at the Chillicothe towns, but was not allowed to talk with him. She said he had been adopted by a widow who had lost a son, and was kindly treated. He never got home, but died in captivity.

Limestone conduits provide us with two never-failing springs fed from the Bullpasture. Springs on the Shenandoah side seep out of shale and are weaker. In drought years they provide only enough water to wash your hands.

From early July until October, the Cowpasture goes underground. Though clear water trickles into long bathtub-deep pools, no water runs out of them and you can walk dry footed across the river between the conical mounds of last spring's fish nests.

Doubtless, the absence of a swimmable stream during the vacation months has deterred second-home builders. Although the Corps of Engineers has eyed this valley for one of their ubiquitous dams, the Corps thought it was too leaky a site, too much trouble.

The Lewises led an expedition against Indian allies of the British in 1768. Though the battle of Point Pleasant was, at best, a Pyrrhic victory (John and Andrew Lewis were both killed), our local historians proudly point to it as the very first battle of the American Revolution. Patrick Miller fought in that command as a ranger and later was awarded a fifty-acre patent for his trouble. The last Indian raid to hit the Cowpasture was in 1774.

Excepting Point Pleasant, the Revolutionary War didn't affect the valley much one way or another. Few of the valley's settlers joined up, battles were fought far away, neither government nor markets were disturbed. The Scotch-Irish settlers and their slaves had started to clear the bottomland and that was enough to keep them busy.

In 1794, Patrick Miller sold his homeplace to John McCorkle, a land speculator, who held it seven years before selling it to James Stuart (William Stuart's son) for 520 pounds, Virginia money.

Many small birds won't fly more than two hundred yards from the safety of the tree canopy. Between mountainside and river, our fields are lined with trees, and bird life is extensive. We have enough wetlands along the river to support wood ducks and attract every year a few migrating geese and, rarely, great blue herons.

This is a verge farm—cultivated land adjacent to wildlife cover—and the farm feeds thousands of creatures besides us and our sheep.

Though the wolves were killed out by 1910 and the last (confirmed) mountain lion was seen in 1912, black bear and bobcats are fairly common. Hunted hard for food and market, by the early twentieth century, the deer population was marginal, but after the State Game Commission was created and passed game laws, deer numbers exploded, and it's hard to watch them in our alfalfa, dozens at a time, without thinking them more nuisance than pleasure. Wild turkeys have been reintroduced in the mountains with great success. Coyotes are reintroducing themselves. Twenty years ago, when we arrived, the county was still paying a bounty on hawks, and they were scarce. In long summer evenings now, I can sit on our front porch and watch redtails riding thermals above the Bullpasture.

*   *   *

Every community has people who embody the community's stories about itself. They are "Native New Yorkers," "Old Village Faces," "Cockneys," "True Parisians." In our valley they're called "Old-Timey."

Everett (Chief) Hupman hunted most days he wasn't fishing or sanging (ginseng gathering). He lived with his cousin Lewis in an asphalt-sided hunt camp. In the fall they'd collect bushels of apples from abandoned orchards, enough to press two barrels—one hundred gallons—of cider. Winter mornings, Chief used to stop here en route to the farm next door, where he'd feed cattle. As the winter deepened and his cider got harder, he wouldn't come off the seat of his Ford 8N tractor—you'd have to go out to him.

One Saturday night, in a local tavern, someone got down on Chief, remarking on his indolent habits. "I am who I am," Chief roared back. "I am a Hupman! That's who I am!"

As early as 1738, when William Stuart set sail from Scotland, highland clans were on the wane. In the mountains of Virginia, vestiges of Scottish clan traditions linger today.

The first settlers brought timothy, orchard grass, herdsgrass (red top). These are cool season grasses, making most of their growth in the spring and fall. The native grasses—big and little bluestem, Indian grass, switch grass, and purple top—are warm-season perennials. Bluestem can grow so tall you can see the man on the tractor mowing it, but not the tractor.

Society in Tidewater Virginia was two-tier: a large number of aristocrats over a much larger base of slaves and servants. A middle strata developed early in the Cowpasture. There were a few great families (the Byrds in this valley, McClintocks and Wallaces in Williamsville). There were small numbers of slaves and laborers. Most of the population—the Stuarts, Millers, Gwins—

belonged to middle-class freeholder households. Typically, each household owned a couple hundred acres of river-bottom land and perhaps five hundred acres of woods. From William Stuart's time until the twentieth century, it was fairly easy to fall in status (most who did so left the county) and almost impossible to rise. The frontier was no democracy.

Williamsville had a mill by 1793 and its blacksmith shop and tannery soon afterward. Schoolmaster William Stuart planted corn, wheat, rye, buckwheat, and barley. He billed three and a third cents a day for schooling and nine cents extra if the scholar boarded with him. He calved cattle, sheared sheep, and, since he had a wagon, made infrequent trips to Staunton for salt, nails, iron, fancy cloth, gunpowder, and tobacco. When a neighbor ran short, he'd get necessaries from Stuart, who'd mark the debt in his account book. When the neighbor made hay for Stuart or brought in firewood, Stuart would credit him fifty cents a day.

Modern industrial peoples locate their security in professions and institutions. Not many doctors get laid off, nor do tenured professors of economics. Postal workers and police officers are safe. If a worker does lose his (her) job, there's unemployment, food stamps, and welfare. None of these programs are well managed or adequate, but they are a safety net William Stuart couldn't have dreamed of. William Stuart was patriarch of the Stuart family, and that family was the sole safety net the Stuarts had. Land, to the Stuarts, was an unsentimental means of production. Good land insured the family's fortune and status.

Modern families are centrifugal. The Stuart family was centripetal.

During his lifetime, William Stuart added to his original holdings by further patents and outright purchase, and at his death he owned some three thousand acres. In his will, he left his Bullpasture farm to his son William, on condition that he "maintain and cloathe sufficiently his younger brother Usher." (I suspect that Usher was retarded, since Stuart's will contains intricate provisions and backup provisions for Usher's lifetime care.) William's "right beloved wife Margaret" got a sorrel mare as well as the use of the homeplace during her widowhood. Daughters (already married) got five pounds and one horse each. James Stuart, the eldest son, got the residual estate. Youngest son John Stuart received the munificent sum of twenty shillings. Two hundred years after the fact, it's not clear what John did to deserve this slap in the face, but we can be reasonably sure he threatened the family's interests, with habitual drunkenness or financial imprudence the most likely threats. Poor, helpless Usher is treated much better than his imprudent brother.

When son James inherited, he was a man of forty with a large family of his own. Traditionally, here, the elder son stayed on the homeplace, gradually increasing his duties and responsibilities as the patriarch aged. During the strongest period of the son's manhood, he had expectations but no legal rights—what if the patriarch and he should have a falling out before the patriarch died?

Besides land, William Stuart left thirteen hogs, twenty-four cows, nine sheep, six horses, a rifle, a loom, a chest, his wagon, one barrel (old), and a few books, but his most valuable possessions— valued at four hundred dollars more than all his other goods put together—were a Negro wench and her child. They were the first black Stuarts.

During the drafting of the Declaration of Independence, the Virginians were quite immoderate—firebrands for freedom. That may have been due to their daily experience with freedom's opposite. Patrick Henry's "Give me liberty or give me death" could be translated "I wouldn't be a slave of mine."

The northern valleys of what became Highland County were settled by Germans, the Cowpasture and Bullpasture valleys by Scotch-Irish. By 1850, the five hundred whites in those two broad southern valleys owned more than half the county's four hundred slaves.

Overseers were never used in this valley, and the Stuarts worked the fields, day in, day out, side by side with their slaves. At the end of the day, they were just as weary, just as dirty, and often ate the same food beside the same fire. Though separate slave quarters were built in the 1830s, before then the family and their slaves wintered in a twelve-by-twelve single-room cabin with an unheated second-story sleeping loft. It must have made for some strange conversations.

Farm work itself was probably not that onerous. The Stuart farm was a self-sufficient, livestock-based operation, and the sheer variety of tasks diminished each one's burden. One day a man might be sowing wheat, the next day hauling stone out of the fields or husking corn. No doubt there'd be days when it was too wet to get into the fields, times when a bear had got into the sheep and needed to be hunted. Whites didn't work on Sundays and, as Christians, blacks didn't either.

After 1800 emigration into this valley slowed, and by 1850, two-thirds of the two hundred fifty people living in the upper Cowpasture had been born here. Families were large: eight or ten children. The boys went to work in the fields as early as they were able to and the girls helped with the household economy.

These farmers had modified their early agricultural practices, but forest farming remained an important part of their husbandry until 1920. After the spring birthing, the animals—cows, sheep, and hogs—were turned into the woods to browse. Though different farmers held patents to parcels on Shenandoah Mountain, the mountain was unfenced and grazed as a common. (Various Virginia enclosure laws were passed in faraway Richmond, but they were routinely ignored here.) In the fall, the farmers brought the livestock out of the woods, and once the leaves fell, they'd burn the woods to eliminate undergrowth and encourage grass. The river bottoms were planted in wheat, corn, barley, rye, oats, and buckwheat. James Stuart sent the family wheat to the Williams- ville Mill (the miller kept an eighth for his fee) and sold the remainder in Staunton. Other grains were fed to the livestock. The Stuarts used honey and maple sugar for sweetener, and ate a great deal of hog meat, dried fruits, corn, and beans. They put up potatoes, apples, and root crops in the root cellars, spun their own wool, loomed their own flax for linen, built icehouses for the ice they sawed out of the rivers.

Since they didn't sell much to the greater economy, they didn't import much either, nor did they use much cash. What kept the Cowpasture economy going was a modified barter system, grounded in the big families. They didn't do simple swaps. If James Stuart wanted William McClintock's tobacco, he gave McClintock a note for the tobacco. McClintock entered the amount in his ledger under "Stuart, James" and later on, perhaps a year or two later, he'd enter "bought three steer hides" and their value, on the other side of the ledger. Men took notes from one another for small amounts—fifty cents, thirty-seven and a half cents—and exchanged them as good as cash. The big families took unto themselves the privilege of issuing currency—a right presently reserved to governments.

For nearly forty years, James Stuart added to the Stuart holdings, patenting still more mountain land and buying out small holders (including the Miller tract). In Stuart's five thousand acres, Miller's land was the farthest from the homeplace at Shaw's Fork, the heart of the Stuart enterprise. On August 28, 1839, James sold it to his eldest son, William R. Stuart, for a thousand dollars: five hundred in cash and a five-hundred-dollar note in hand. It was an odd transaction.

When William R. Stuart moved here, this land had been farmed at a distance for thirty years by Stuarts (and their slaves), who'd made the eight-mile trip from Shaw's Fork to get their work done. Farming at a distance doesn't work well today and would have worked less well in the nineteenth century. I think that by 1839 not much would have changed on Patrick Miller's farm—the important cleared fields, still Miller's fields, against the Shenandoah Mountain, stumps in the river bottom where James Stuart's slaves had felled the trees.

In 1973 I talked to Connor Gillespie, a hundred years old then, and he told me what his great-great-grandfather had told him when he was a boy: "All them black walnut trees, tremendous trees, they'd never been cut before, you see. They just felled them and piled 'em up and put a torch to 'em."

William R. Stuart moved his family (and two slaves) into Miller's sixty-year-old one-room dirt-floored cabin, repaired Miller's ramshackle barns and hog pens, and commenced to farm.

Perhaps William R. left Shaw's Fork because he was getting impatient: The old man was eighty-two and showing no signs of dropping the reins. Perhaps William R. and old James simply had a falling-out.

Two years later, when the old man did die, he left William R. Stuart "the plantation on which he presently resides, providing he pays the remaining five hundred dollars." To rub salt in the wound, his father bequeathed William R. the sum of one dollar. William's brother St. Clair got the bulk of the land, the farming implements, William's note, and all the patriarchal duties. St. Clair was to provide for Usher (elderly now) and give him a decent burial. He was to keep his mother, Jane Stuart, in meat and wheat and firewood and find pasture for her personal livestock.

To his wife, James Stuart also left the furniture, the beds and bedding, her choice of two horses, four cows, ten sheep, the use of the homeplace, its orchard, stable, and barn, and the use of negro Harry, negresses Hannah and Beloy, for her lifetime. As these early wills show, it was the patriarch's task to provide for his wife, not give up control. Wives rarely inherited, but were never left unprovided for.

Among his possessions, James Stuart also left a library of books to be divided among his sons.

*   *   *

Limestone, as I've said, is water soluble, and the fields right below the Bullpasture are more or less self-liming. Because of underground seeps and high rainfall, the river fields are acid, and every couple of years we must haul in loads of ground limestone to sweeten the soil and keep it productive.

It was Edmund Ruffin, in 1818, who discovered the chemistry of Virginia soil and the advantages of "Marling." Ruffin set his slaves to excavate limestone rock and spread it across his fields, and, miraculously, fields that had been "exhausted" came back into fertility. Ruffin published "An essay on calcerous manures" in 1832 and founded *The Farmer's Register* to promote his agricultural reforms.

Though liming was his great discovery, Ruffin also proselytized for manuring, draining, deep plowing, and crop rotation. Tidewater Virginia's "exhausted" land sprang back to life under his suggestions, and his *Farmer's Register* was soon the most influential agricultural journal in the southeast. In 1810, when Peru began exporting guano from its offshore seabird colonies, Virginia farmers possessed every element of an agricultural boom: good markets, cheap fertility, and (in slaves) cheap power. It was slaves, of course, who dug the limestone, broke it up, hauled it, and spread it. Ruffin claimed that his practices combined "science and slavery." In 1832, the Virginia legislature failed to abolish slavery by a handful of votes. (The Stuarts' representative voted for abolition.) The debate would never be so close again. Edmund Ruffin had demonstrated that Virginia planters needed their slaves. And, in 1861, he had the great honor of firing the first shot at Fort Sumpter.

By the 1840s, Ruffin's practices had reached the Shenandoah Valley—*The Farmer's Register* had subscribers there—and though Cowpasture farmers knew about liming in 1860, none limed their land until well after the war.

William R. Stuart added mountain land to his holdings: 208

acres in 1843, parcels of 195 acres and 144 acres the following year. He was patenting the common land nobody else wanted (it was valued at ten cents an acre), and the Stuart farm climbed up Shenandoah Mountain to Brushy Fork, on both sides of the jerkemtight trail.

William R. built slave quarters beside the river to house six slaves: female blacks, aged forty, twenty-three, and twelve, and males, aged eighteen, ten, and three. Although Stuart was no slave dealer, his slaves were never guaranteed a lifetime on the farm, and he occasionally bought and sold the people he worked beside, people who, like his own children, were born and raised here on this remote farm tucked between the looming mountains. Sundays, the Stuarts went to church in Williamsville. The blacks went too, though as the ninety-five-year-old daughter of a slave told me, "We had to sit in the garret." They entered by a separate door and climbed into the balcony.

Robert Lockridge and Franklin McClintock lived downriver from the Stuart farm; the Gwins, upriver.

July the 12th 1847

Mr. Lockridge, dear Sir, I embrace the present opportunity to write a few lines to let you know that I am well at this time. I hope that those few lines may reach you enjoying the same health. I have no news to write you more than I expect that my wife will be Sold in the Fall if you or your brother David don't do something for me I expect that we will be parted. I want you to come and buy us both & if you can you will do me a great favor. I want you to answer this letter if you please and you will much oblige your humble servant, for wife & me have lived together for many years & would like to live with you again if it will meet with your approbation. Give my best respects to all inquiring friends. Nothing more but to remain your obedient servant

Isaac Gwin, servant
of Franklin McClintock

Farm laborers, free and slave, were usually illiterate, transient, and excepting brief appearances in criminal court records, left few traces in the valley. The Stuart family graveyard is an overgrown brush heap at the foot of Shaw's Ridge. The crude headstones are unmarked limestone and sandstone slabs. I have no idea where the Stuart slaves were buried.

Bordering our hill field, just beneath the Bullpasture, is a substantial stone wall laid up of limestone rocks dragged out of that bottom. In these mountains, fences were made of split chestnut rails, and stone walls are scarce. I think Jared Stuart, William R.'s son, built that wall in 1860, helped by his father's slaves. I think that one of those slaves was named James and that he was thirteen when he helped lever and grunt those stones into place. We shall meet James again, after emancipation.

Female slaves worked in the house as "servants"—a word that connoted more necessity than it does today. These women were not ladies' maids. They worked beside the Stuart women in the domestic economy, gathering the eggs, making butter and cheese, helping milk the Stuarts' nine milk cows, salting down and turning the hog meat, brining the beef, making the soap, spinning the wool, looming the flax, drying the summer produce, nursing the sick and feeble. Although the men plowed the garden, planting, weeding, and harvesting were jobs reserved for women and children. The first loads of manure from the horse and milk-cow barns went onto the garden soils. What was left over was spread on the crop lands. Stuart men planted "Old Mediterranean" wheat and oats in the fall and corn in the spring, boiled maple syrup in the spring and gathered honey after the October frost. In 1850, William R. Stuart owned seven horses, twenty-five cows (plus his milk cows), forty-five sheep, and thirty-five hogs, at a total value of $855.

Stuart made eighty bushels of wheat that year and three hundred bushels of Indian corn (which fed his stock and, after being ground into meal in Williamsville, fed his family). He put up forty tons of hay, made one hundred bushels of flax, three hundred pounds of maple sugar, ten gallons of sorghum molasses, and one hundred pounds of honey.

Although some progressive Shenandoah Valley farmers were importing British bloodstock to improve their cattle and sheep, mountain farmers preferred smaller, hardier, adapted animals. In any event, common grazing would have prevented any improvements. Their full-grown cows weighed between seven hundred and nine hundred pounds, sheep less than fifty. On a spring day, a hundred forty years later, I helped an old-fashioned mountain farmer shear his sheep. I could catch full-grown beasts and tuck them under my arm.

William R. Stuart built himself a two-story log house, covered with clapboard, with a great stone chimney. Seated on its covered porch, a prosperous man could oversee all he owned: the barns, the springhouse, the orchard, the slave quarters, his fertile fields.

By 1860, the farm was valued at five thousand dollars—after the Byrd place, at the mouth of the valley, the most valuable farm on the upper Cowpasture. Farming is sometimes said to be an "easy access" profession. In 1860, a farm laborer was paid fifty cents for the day's work that nets forty dollars today. The laborer in 1860 would have needed to save every cent he earned for thirty-two years to buy this farm. In 1990, it would take him twelve years of saving. The farm isn't worth what it was.

By 1860, Jared Stuart had left his father's house, moved across the river into the hundred-year-old Miller cabin, and started his own family. He and William R. farmed together, and when one man spoke, he spoke for the other.

There's a tintype of Jared from about this period. He's a tiny, hot-eyed man in a suit two sizes too big for him. For some reason —nervousness? cockiness?—he stands with one foot underneath the other.

In the presidential election of 1860, Highland County voted

for Stephen Douglas, the "moderate" northern candidate. County politicos opposed secession until, after Sumter, Lincoln announced plans to send troops into the South. Neighboring Pocohontas County and Pendleton County broke away with West Virginia for the Union, but Highland joined the Confederacy. Highland's rivers flowed into the James to Richmond. Her markets lay south. There was surprisingly little debate: A handful of citizens opted for the Union, but hundreds fought for the Confederacy.

In the spring of 1862, Federal troops, under General Robert Milroy, came into Highland County and, on April 24, sent a forage party to Williamsville. Although the foragers found what they came for—corn, wheat, and flour—the river came up and they couldn't return home immediately. John T. Byrd galloped to Rockbridge Alum Springs, where a Confederate cavalry detachment was encamped. Some forty Confederates rode through the night, and by dawn on the 26th, they were east of Williamsville, athwart the road the Yankees would use. Tower Hill is steep, a hard pull for horses and wagons, and when the foragers and soldier escort made the top, they rested. One Confederate thought the Yanks were spooked: "They were looking around uneasily like so many wild turkeys." A ragged volley announced the hostilities and, soon enough, those Federals not wounded or captured were in flight. The Confederates wrecked the wagons and withdrew.

The regulars were assisted in this attack by a number of local citizens, perhaps including Jared Stuart, but nobody boasted about his participation when angry Federals reoccupied the town with three companies of troops. Soldiers were posted at the McClintock place, the Wallace place, the Byrd farm, and the Presbyterian church. After riding horses through the church, they boasted that they had "taken their horses to prayer meeting." They hunted but failed to find John T. Byrd. When they retired to McDowell, they took civilian hostages with them, but these were soon released. On May 8, 1862, when Stonewall Jackson defeated Union forces at the

Battle of McDowell, the distant rumble of cannon sounded, to local farmers, very much like deliverance.

So many men enlisted and so many slaves escaped that by 1863, Elizabeth Gum wrote her son, "There is not men here enough to support the population and if there is not a change for the better and that soon, starvation must ensue." They had no salt or wheat, and corn was "7–9$ a bushel and none to be had." Their animals were suffering, "poorer brutes you never seen walk on the earth."

The war killed two of William R. Stuart's sons—James and Ferdinand—and widowed his daughter Susan. But the worst blow was the epidemic that swept through the valley in the summer of 1862—Mrs. Gum calls it "slave fever" and says, "it appears in defiance of medicine." The fever killed William R. Stuart's wife and two of his grandchildren (Jared's children).

In 1865, William R. remarried—Elizabeth Bennett, widowed in the final year of the war. When I asked the Stuarts which battle killed Bennett, they handed me one of those family explanations, a sentence that has passed through the generations, perfect and intact. "Oh, he was just slippin' away to join his family, and one of his own sentries shot him," Marie Stuart said. "Isn't that just awful?"

Despite war, despite the loss of its slaves, in 1870 the Stuart farm was more prosperous than ever. Stuart had more livestock, more machinery, and more money. He had a hired man, John Fogolin. Daughter Elizabeth was living in the main house with her husband, Floyd Kincaid. Son Jared, now fifty, had taken over most of his sickly father's farming duties.

Most of the freed Stuart slaves left the mountains. Others, including James and John Stuart, stayed and found work wherever they could. Before the war, Edmund Ruffin had calculated that it cost seventy-eight dollars per year to keep a slave. Since a twenty-year-old slave cost eight hundred dollars and lasted until he was about forty, you can add another forty-dollar yearly depreciation to that figure. After the war, a ruined Edmund Ruffin learned of the wages offered black entrants in the free-labor market. "If labor could have been hired and commanded at the highest of these rates," he wrote, "I would, for economy, have ceased to be a slave owner fifty years ago." Soon afterward, Ruffin shot himself.

In 1868, freed slave James Stuart went to work on the nearby McClintock farm for a hundred and eight dollars per year. Against his account, they charged all goods and services fronted him.

Jan. 18	½ bushel meal	.38
	38 lbs. beef	2.66
	1 bag wool	1.00
Jan. 23	1 plug tobacco	.45
Jan. 26	1 day lost, Thos Wallace	
	1 day lost, hauling wood	

They sold the ex-slave sugar, tobacco, corn, wheat, whiskey, and shoe leather. They paid his small notes to G. W. MacDonald and Dr. Armstrong. They deducted every day he worked for himself or hired out to others, docked him in June the day he went to a sale, the half-day he went to the election. Docked him a day and a half on July 16 and 17 when his child was born, and docked him two days, August 6 and 7, spent burying it.

In 1873, William R. Stuart's farm was rich. His apple trees were Black Twig, Baldwin, and the yellow apples called in the north "Newtown" Pippin but known locally as the "Albemarle" Pippin. He probably grew the postwar apple: Jefferson Davis. This apple was mealy, tough skinned, and not very flavorful, but, it was said, it kept forever.

His garden grew blood turnip beets, earliest express cabbage, Maul's earliest tomato, evergreen broom corn, white plume celery, cucumber, gourds, yellow globe danver onions, french asparagus beans, Florida favorite watermelon and Dixie watermelon, early nutmeg muskmelon, and Maul's Superior enormous tomato.

He also grew peaches: Crawford Early, Sallie Worrell, Susquehanna, Crawford's late Monstrous Ponfone, Foster, Governor Wood, and Early Richmond. He grew Seconte and Keifer pears.

But western wheat was flooding eastern markets and the wheat price wouldn't climb above a dollar a bushel again until the First World War. The Panic of 1873 closed banks and manufacturies all over the nation.

During William R.'s final illness, his daughter, Elizabeth Stuart Kincaid, and her husband, Floyd, tended the dying old man. Son Jared stayed in the fields.

For two years after his death, the old man commanded, the Kincaids and Stuarts were to share the farm—"peaceably" if possible. Floyd and Elizabeth would live in the house. After two years, the land would be sold. Daughter Elizabeth got all the sheep and hogs, the household goods, her choice of the horses and cattle, plus eleven hundred dollars in cash. After various other bequests, none larger than two hundred dollars, the residue went to Jared.

It looks as though Elizabeth and feisty Jared didn't get along. Elizabeth is supposed to have been a rather fat woman. She appears in local business ledgers frequently, and since this is unusual for an unwidowed woman, I presume she was unusually able. One day, while crossing the river on Williamsville's rickety ferry, Elizabeth slipped and was pitched overboard. Husband Floyd cried out, "Oh, my Honey Pet! I've lost my Honey Pet!"

Three years later, to satisfy his father's will, Jared Stuart sold the farm to a half brother and bought it back the same day. He sold off some mountain land and sixty acres of prime river bottom, including his father's big house, barns, springhouse, orchard, smithy, and sawmill, to a valley newcomer, J. S. Hupman. Hupman is recent enough there are stories about him. He was said to be a wonderful penman, a real calligrapher. It's said he was paranoid and wealthy, burying money in jars up on the mountain somewhere.

What Jared Stuart retained of his inheritance is our farm of today. In the river bottom Jared Stuart fenced five fields, none larger than eighteen acres. We call them the "Big River," "Little River," "Hill Field," and "Big and Little Triangle" fields. The long field on the far side of the river (Miller's), Jared Stuart cropped in corn. Because we no longer use it, the field has lost its name.

The house Jared Stuart built in 1877, a one-room log cabin with sleeping loft, is now our living room. The two-story addition he put on later, also log, is our library and upstairs bedroom. The bank barn he built has room for hay storage above and animal quarters below. It is spanned by three forty-foot sills, each hewn from a single yellow pine. Designed originally for loose hay, we store between two and three thousand fifty-pound bales of hay there for the winter. Below, using movable partitions, we contain our ewes at shearing time and during lambing, we keep twenty-four ewes and lambs in individual pens on one side and use the other side for a communal nursery. That's when it's best in the barn, on a cold November night, when meteor Kamikazes are diving out of the Milky Way. Inside, the barn is a snug hotel for sheep. Their body heat (and all that insulating hay overhead) keep the barn twenty degrees warmer than the outside, as the animals sleep and ruminate and moan and fart and dream on their beds of golden straw. It seems right, like we've done something properly for a change.

Numerous small seeps in our river fields, below the Bullpasture, suggest the presence of a sandstone layer, like a baker's tray underneath the subsoil. This water cannot be intercepted by diversion ditches at the base of the mountain, and water bubbling onto thick clay soil is troublesome. It's hard to get into the fields for early planting and most legumes don't like wet feet.

In the wintertime, when snow dusts the bare ground, Jared Stuart's solution to this problem becomes visible. He plowed his fields in long, narrow rectangles, heaping the soil from outside to middle, creating thousand-foot-long, thirty-foot-wide raised beds which stay above the water. Grass ditches between the beds take water to wetlands beside the river. Edmund Ruffin's essay "The advantages of plowing land in wide beds" was published in *The American Farmer* in 1851.

Jared's horse-drawn plow and mower had a very short turning radius. Modern machinery is designed to follow the field perimeter in ever diminishing squares. Modern machinery has unsolved Jared Stuart's solution. Today's fields are too wet to plant, and every time I cross one of those old ditches on my tractor, my teeth rattle.

Jared Stuart was the first farmer to lime these fields, using burnt lime from the Byrd family lime kiln, a half mile down the road.

Despite his efforts, the value of the Stuart place plummeted. Land worth twenty-six dollars an acre when he inherited it was worth half that when he passed it on.

In Columbus, Ohio, in the spring of 1971, I paid five hundred dollars for a six-year-old International pickup and another hundred for a tool box and socket set from Sears. I built a rather jolly canvas camper on the back of the truck. Anne and I planned to travel north from the Smokies, seeking a piece of land with wildlife and clean water. As it turned out, the first requirement was easy, the second nearly impossible. Clean water is rare.

In Kentucky's highest mountains, the streams ran yellow with acid leachate from the strip mines. Toilet paper festooned streamside bushes, and the murky creeks sluiced over the snouts of abandoned cars. In some of the coal towns the only viable small businesses were used-car lots: reliable getaway vehicles brought a premium. I thought then that a ruined land makes ruined people, that it is probably impossible to create human community on a Superfund site. Given the thoroughness of environmental destruction in this country, my view is inevitably elitist. It is no accident that we contain our poor on barren Indian reservations or the brick-strewn streets of the South Bronx. Only educated whites are allowed to escape the consequences of what educated whites have created.

There are several reasons our farm has clean water, none especially edifying. We are fairly close to the headwaters springs. Roads into the county are uniformly bad. Though the Chamber of Commerce and other forward-thinking citizens here have begged industry to come and set up shop, provide employment and paychecks, so far industry has declined this offer, preferring to ruin the water of communities with better roads. And there's never been much in Highland County worth stealing. We lack coal and other minerals, there's no oil. The best timber was taken off in the early twenties.

The great dream of capitalism is "Get Rich and Get Out." Make your pile, rip your wealth out of a community, and bundle it off to Paradise, where you can suck on mint juleps and the servants will call you sir.

More and more rich folks settle in this county every year.

In 1898, when Worthy B. Stuart inherited this land from Jared, the population of Highland was 5,000 people, of whom only 132 couldn't read or write. The Byrds sent their sons to private school at nearby Bath Alum, where they studied Greek and Latin as well as German and French. Cattle and sheep populations were 10,000 and 20,000 respectively. Six hundred fifteen of the county's 679 farms were mortgage free. The *Baltimore Sun* and *Philadelphia Inquirer* offered subscriptions here. Philadelphia buggy makers and implements dealers sought farmer custom. Drovers brought herds of cattle into the county, took other batches out. Monterey, the county seat, boasted a brass band.

But in the early twenties, Worthy B. Stuart was presented with opportunities his forebears never dreamed of.

Having logged the Michigan hardwoods, lumber companies discovered the Allegheny highlands with their great forests of virgin oak, hickory, maple, and chestnut. Lumber companies offered to buy land and stumpage. They offered employment at salaries greater than a farmer could pay (or earn, for that matter).

Lawsuits erupted over conflicting patents issued while Virginia was still an English colony. That mountain land was valuable. Worthy B. Stuart sold coal rights, timber rights, even a right-of-way to a railroad (never built) to cross the river. When all the timber was gone and the federal government came seeking land for its National Forest system, he sold that, too. That wasn't entirely his doing; lawyers tied him in knots and the government threatened to condemn what he didn't wish to sell. Although the government stopped the farmer's traditional autumn woods burning, they could continue to graze livestock as they always had for another ten years. And surely the government would renew the grazing rights, wouldn't they? They didn't.

Since 1760, this farm had fed, clothed, and housed seventy human beings through all the days of their lives. It had helped sustain a church, a gristmill, a community. Thousands of cattle, sheep, and hogs had grazed here. The farm had endured financial panics, wars, and numerous agricultural hard times.

Wes Jackson speaks of "things which once possessed cannot be done without," and it was lumber money, the pleasures of mobility (the automobile), and the loss of the woodlands that destroyed this farm. The soil was still good, the buildings sound, no erosion at all when the Stuarts moved off the farm in 1929 and into town. The farm was tenanted by different sharecroppers until 1940, when Mrs. E. B. Mackey (she'd grown up next door) bought it for thirty-four hundred dollars. Mr. Mackey was the Williamsville miller, and when the FDA closed most country gristmills in the late forties, he turned to carpentry for a living. He enclosed the long shaded front porch for a kitchen and dining room. The

Mackeys farmed a bit and took in dozens of deer hunters during the season. In 1966, Mrs. Mackey, widowed, moved off the farm. Farm and farmhouse were empty, abandoned.

Although Worthy B. Stuart wasn't a very good farmer, it wasn't personal failure that pushed the Stuarts off a land they'd held for more than a century. Down the road, the better-off Byrds sold out, too, and when the roof blew off the Miller house (now the Robinson Lockridge place), Robinson just moved downstairs where the rain couldn't get to him. When the roof came off the J. S. Hupman house (William R. Stuart's homeplace), nobody bothered to replace that either.

The promises that had kept these families in the upper Cowpasture had gone stale in the mouth and they sought new promises elsewhere. Those few who stayed reverted to the hunting, fishing, gathering patterns of their pre-Revolutionary War ancestors.

The fences fell down, cedars crept back into the fields, one by one the churches and schools closed. In 1948, the rural electric brought power to this valley. 1948 was the last year there were children for the school-bus run.

Occasionally, Miss Marie Stuart and her sister Lilian return to visit the farm their family left fifty years ago. When I worked the Headwaters' precinct elections, I met old Weldon Stuart, of the Shaw's Ridge Stuarts. At eighty-eight, Weldon was our oldest voter.

All the Stuarts have high, broad foreheads, high cheekbones, sharp noses, small jaws. You can see what the early Stuarts looked like, though Marie and Weldon's common ancestor, James Stuart, died in 1841.

The Stuarts were intelligent, careful farmers who played a smaller role in county affairs than their status would suggest. They never served as slave patrollers, were never magistrates or justices of the peace. Only William R. Stuart was a deacon in the church.

They named their children St. Clair and Ferdinand and Rennick. They read books. Worthy Stuart's wife, Lena, had been raised to be a pianist and never did housework or cooked a meal until she came to the lonely farmhouse in the valley. Local legend says that Weldon Stuart's wife was so shy, she climbed into the apple tree and hid when she saw visitors coming, and when she cooked supper for the threshing crews, they'd come into the dining room to find their places set, all the food out in steaming bowls and platters, and they'd never catch a glimpse of the woman who'd made their meal.

Whatever the Stuarts found here in this valley satisfied them for a very long time, and when it didn't, they left, as quietly as they came.

Describing ignorance is like defining God: One is soon reduced to negative definition. We didn't know this about the farm, we didn't know that about country living, we hadn't a clue . . .

In June of 1971, we drove down the farm lane for the first time. Three horses grazed in the yard. It was a bright afternoon and the big field below the house had been cut for hay. The fields seemed big. Big in an intimidating way. The realtor pointed at the broken pear tree, the apple trees, noted the black walnuts that shaded the lane.

I remember that we walked down to the river, cupped our hands and drank sweet water. On the far bank, we passed the site of the original Miller homestead: nothing there now but a flat place, an old dead apple tree with a salt bag attached to its branches. Underneath, the deer had pawed through the soil to bedrock after the salt drippings. We followed the old logging road, up past the place where they'd had their sawmill in 1920. The white pines were just fifty years old, but they were too big for me to encircle with my arms.

There wasn't a fence on the place, the horse barn was beyond repair, the hay barn was coming up the hill, but that evening, before we left, the mists had begun to collect in the hollows, like smoke from ghost campfires.

The very last day I lived in Manhattan was September 11, 1971. It was one of those days. In certain light, in the fall, New York City is airy and spacious, fragile and free. Because Greenwich Village keeps to human scale, the light thrives there and dirty old Cornelia Street can seem gracious. We'd given up our apartment, and our scanty furniture was loaded in the U-Haul parked in New Jersey behind Anne's folks' garage. I'd come into town, one last time, to have lunch with an advertising friend, buy three pair of good wool socks, and withdraw our life's savings, some ten thousand dollars, from the bank. I'd never seen a thousand-dollar-bill before.

We had lunch at the Rivera, at their outdoor café facing Sheridan Square, and it was a long, liquid lunch. By four o'clock I was sad to leave this beautiful city, my fascinating advertising career, all my warm fellow employees. And what about this sunlight?

Soon the sunlight began to fade and my friend had to go back uptown to his office and I wandered around the Village, smashed and maudlin. It wasn't a good idea, not with ten grand in my pocket, but I was probably trying to screw things up. I did lose my new socks, set them down someplace and some thief spirited them away.

Two days later, we bumped down the lane to an abandoned farmhouse surrounded by knee-deep grass. It was me and Anne, her friend Marsha, who'd stay only a couple of weeks, and Richard Simon, who'd stay almost a year. Since the dining room window looked out at the mountains, that's where we put our table. The house boasted sixty watts of power. No phone. There was no phone line in the valley.

Though there was a pipe from the pump to the kitchen sink, the pump hadn't worked in years. We caught water under the downspout. Glass was out of the windows and the roof leaked. We tore the tin covering off the fireplace in the living room, lit a fire, spread our sleeping bags on the floor, and were warmed like Jared Stuart had been, a hundred years ago.

Through October, we haunted the farm auctions looking for cheap furniture, hand tools, and wood stoves. We paid five dollars for one parlor stove, seven-fifty for another. We found our cook stove at an auction outside Monterey. At eleven o'clock, they auctioned the house and a hundred acres, and in the afternoon they sold the horse-drawn rake and mower, the grindstone, the porch swings, the buckets of splines for maple sugaring, and the sugar buckets. Our stove was heating the sugar house when we bidders followed the auctioneer inside: "I've got ten, ten, do I hear fifteen?" People joked about the snow flying in the air, how food cooked on wood heat tasted better, how it was just like the stove Mother used (not *my* mother—*my* mother cooked with electricity). "Do I hear twenty?"

We bought our cookstove, a Montgomery Ward Windsor, for twenty-five dollars, but had to wait until morning when it cooled to pick it up. By then, there were four inches of snow on the ground.

We bought a new pump and it took me a week to figure out how to install it. From then on, except when the line was frozen, we had cold water in our kitchen. What a luxury it is, not hauling water, having a tap right inside the house. Marsha left for California. Every day Simon and I climbed Bullpasture Mountain for our firewood. I wore Mr. Mackey's old flannel-lined jacket I'd found hanging in the barn. We cut big dead oaks into baulks with the chainsaw and rolled them downhill, one man spotting for approaching cars because some of those wood wheels would careen down the mountainside like juggernauts. When one great round baulk took a bad bounce and creamed our truck's back fender, Simon thought it was funny. Not me.

It is a great pleasure to do work that is directly necessary, to cut wood you'll burn, to stuff rags where the glass is out, and keep your hot water boiling on the wood stove. In the wee hours after the fires died out, the kitchen dropped below zero, so we stored our beer in the refrigerator, where it wouldn't freeze.

In early October I started mailing Thanksgiving invitations. I sent letters to all the people who'd worked on that Maine cabin, and a couple who hadn't. We tore ugly wallpaper off the wood-plank walls, inspected and patched the chimneys, and installed a tin stove in the big room that used to be the parlor, thinking our guests could sleep in there. After breakfast, we'd take a long walk in the woods across the river. It was so beautiful—once they saw it, surely some other couple would come in with us.

We met old Peewee Stevenson, who had made hay that summer and stored it in our barn, and every other morning he'd drive in and I'd help him load his pickup. At the time Peewee was seventy and I was thirty and he loaded two bales to my one.

The preacher came down to invite us to a revival. We said, No thanks, we're not Christians, and he said, Why, then, this is just the thing for you.

It got colder. We had bags and bags of organic grains stored in the root cellar. We had almost two thousand dollars' cash money. By stringing blankets between the living room and dining room, we had one room warm enough to take our coats off. The kitchen water line usually thawed by noon.

It got dark by six o'clock.

One by one, invited guests sent back regrets. The "maybe"s turned into "sorry"s. Anne had bought a seventeen-pound turkey, ten pounds of sweet potatoes, and several gallons of cranberries. The last "maybe" turned into "no" the day before Thanksgiving.

When the three of us sat down for Thanksgiving dinner, the snow was sweeping down the broad valley, in curtains, more gray than white. The wind bent the dead yellow broomsage. It'd be warmer in here if we hung drapes over the black glass windows. Anne brought in the turkey. Thank you, Lord, for the gifts we are about to receive.

PART II

Farming

What
Do I Owe
You?

This is what one Highland County farmer told me: "I own the place outright. Got a strong spring, oak trees for firewood, and saw timber. In March we tap the maples for syrup, and my wife, she keeps bees—I'm scared to death of the pesky things. See those peach trees on the hill? The apples? Those black/whiteface steers in the meadow are mine and the sheep on yonder hill." The old farmer laughed. "It makes a man pretty hard to get along with."

Highland is one of Virginia's poor counties. Most of the farms have been in the same families since the Civil War, and not many earn more than ten thousand dollars a year. Don't get me wrong; people aren't poor. They've got plenty to eat. Clothes might be out of style but they're clean. A 1968 Ford F-100 pickup will get you to all the same places a new BMW can. But cash is scarce.

Pride and scant cash is an awkward combination.

Suppose you do someone a service: loan your jumper cables,

pluck his truck out of the ditch. He'll go straight for his wallet: "What do I owe you?"

"Nothing at all."

"You sure?" That painfully thin wallet in his hand. "I'd be happy to pay."

Our neighbor Robert Lockridge was failing. He'd had two heart attacks and the gray color of his face made his neighbors afraid. But Robert wouldn't quit working. He put in twenty acres of oats every spring and picked eight acres of corn every fall. He picked every ear by hand.

Robert didn't have any help except his grandsons, ten and twelve years old. Whenever hot work was nigh, Robert's wife would phone me, whispering so he wouldn't overhear: "Do you think you could happen by?"

It was August, ninety-five degrees, and hard to take breath. Me and Robert's grandkids on the hay wagon and Robert on the tractor. *Ka-chunk, ka-chunk;* the old baler spit out the bales.

When we stopped for a drink of cool water from the jug, Robert's face looked awful. I said, "Me and the boys can finish up this field. Why don't you sit in the shade and supervise?"

He said, "I guess I'll keep working so long as I am able."

After we bucked the last bales up into the barn loft, we jumped and skidded down the hay: healthy young animals. Old, frail Robert Lockridge reached for his wallet. "How much do I owe you?"

"I..."

"You been doin' right smart of work for me, Mr. McCaig, and I guess I'll pay you."

The twenty dollars he gave me was more money to him than it was to me. But twenty dollars can be big money sometimes. I knew just enough to take it, with thanks. It would have shamed him if I'd said no.

Fences

Without good fences, no farmer can enjoy his animals. There is nothing more hateful than sheep in the alfalfa unless it's cows in the corn.

Our oldest fence is the stone wall above the hill field; slaves built that. Wherever animals get pressed, in corrals or chutes, we have board fences. In the very heart of Anne's vegetable garden is a thirty-foot square of yellow mesh electric fence surrounding the new peas and salad greens. We are generally willing to share our food, but no creature eats the new peas who can't write a thank-you note. Our field fences are high-tensile wire, taut as guitar strings on posts twenty feet apart. High tensile is cheap and goes up quick, and three years ago, when floodwaters took out a mile of fence along the river, it took three men two weeks to replace it.

We've got a few stretches of rusty woven wire with two strands of barbwire stretched above. It'll contain cows or sheep. Woodchucks and rabbits go through it, dogs go under, deer jump. Sometimes a deer makes a miscalculation and this fence can kill it.

If a deer jumps a little low, slips a hind foot between those two strands of barbwire, the wire wraps that leg tighter than handcuffs. The deer hangs upside down on the far side of the fence until it dies.

Last August, Anne spotted something white against the triangle field fence. Milkweed? Puff of tattered baling twine? We were in a rush to go to town, so it wasn't until dusk we put the binoculars on the white thing she'd seen.

It was a deer's belly, a young buck with first horns not yet formed. What they call a "button buck." When I lifted it so Anne could snip the wire off its legs, it didn't weigh seventy pounds. They're not very big, you know. All wild things look bigger than they are.

Frightened deer bleat, just like a lamb.

I slung the deer around my neck and carried him down next to the woods. Anne clipped some grass for him. She left drinking water in an old plastic bowl.

He'd hung there since the night before, ruining tendons, tearing ligaments, and I wasn't very hopeful. Next morning, when I went down to check on him, I carried my gun. He'd managed to drag himself about twenty yards from the water dish.

I spoke to him, explaining that pretty soon the foxes and coyotes would find him. I said I was sorry, too.

At my shot, ravens started cawing in the woods and I saw a deer flag. Another. Another deer, another. Slowly, a dozen deer bounced away into the forest. I believe they were friends of his. I believe they kept by him during the night and waited until I came to say good-bye.

Market

You northerners remember last December when it was twenty below and the radio warning people to please stay indoors? We had a hundred thirty lambs on the ground. Most of the lambs could stand the cold, but orphan lambs are always weaker than the others, so we brought six of them in the house. Anne set up a wooden lamb pen down in our sun room, bedded it with straw, and they were snug as bugs. They were surprisingly quiet, very rarely baaed. Our sheep dogs walked by without looking at them. *Lambs in the House???* Sheep dogs hate disorder. We kept them inside a week, until the cold weather broke.

Last week I took those lambs to market. Without fail, the night before we load lambs, Anne and I get real grouchy. She's the one with the day-to-day care of them, so it's me has to drive them in.

We get up at daybreak, grab a cup of coffee, and get out there before we have to think too much. The dogs crowd all the lambs into a pen and we sort off twenty-three big ones. Lambs don't like to go anywhere unfamiliar, and they've never been in our loading chute, never been on a truck. I'm pretty sure they know what's in store for them. They know we're predators. We've got an old deaf sheep dog whose only job, year in and year out, is loading lambs. We won't let them turn back or break past her. She is calm and implacable.

We are especially gentle today, soft spoken. It is important not to sic the dogs on, not to lose patience with animals on their way to slaughter. It's hard enough to kill an animal; it is indecent to be unkind.

Once the truck gets moving, the lambs settle down. I drive real slow and traffic backs up behind me. Coming down the mountain, I gear down.

I've seen what happens when a stock truck has an accident.

On every turn, the truck tilts when the lambs find new footing.

At the stock market, I unload, chivvy them through dim wooden corridors to the scale, where the grader runs his hands down their backs. Twenty of our lambs grade blue—that's the top grade—and three are reds. We make $1,427 for those animals. That's $62 apiece.

When the price is better, it feels better bringing them in, but lamb prices are off this year about thirty percent. They won't be off, of course, at your local supermarket. After raising and tending these lambs for six months, we get two dollars for the lamb chops that cost you nine. I haven't figured how we'll make out this year raising livestock, but if it's like most years, it won't be minimum wage.

Some days it isn't much fun either.

Rabies

There's been rabies in the county recently. Up by Blue Grass, Bob Rexrode lost a dog to it and Joe Malcolm from Doe Hill had a bull that got infected. You hardly ever hear of large stock getting rabies, and it's especially troublesome because suppose *your* bull comes up sick, well, the first thing you do is start pushing pills down his throat and rabies spreads by saliva.

In January I shot a rabid fox and last week let a skunk live that I probably shouldn't have. It's no mercy: Their nerve synapses are firing like firecrackers, they feel awful, what was real isn't real anymore, they don't know who their enemies are.

Last Sunday morning, I took Silk out for a walk. Since Silk is half-deaf, she's not much use as a sheep dog, and since Silk was in heat, I couldn't exercise her with the other dogs. Silk was happy to be out, sniffing her sniffs, enjoying my undivided attention. She saw the fox first.

It was a young red fox, just beyond the garden fence, eighty yards from the house, exposed, in broad daylight, trotting along completely unafraid.

There's a country rule about foxes: If you see one, it's rabid. Silk headed right for it, tail awag. "Silk, that'll do! Silk, here! SILK!" And I stood where she could see me if she looked back, poor deaf bitch, so I could wave her off the damn thing. The fox didn't fret as Silk came near, her tail stiffening, head lowering toward the ground: What is this? What is this?

Miraculously, Silk looked back, and with every inch of my body, I invited her to come to me, and when she came, the rabid fox followed her, pretty quick, and I backed up pretty quick. Though Silk has had rabies shots, I haven't.

I ran with Silk to the house and snatched the .22 and ran back outside, and a hundred of our sheep had come over to investigate the sick, fearless little thing. Nose to nose, fox to sheep, they were, and some ewes were pawing the ground and others wanted to play. I guess they thought it was a barn cat. Thirty feet away, I couldn't shoot without hitting a sheep, and I daren't bring out a sheepdog to move them. "Sheeby, sheeby, here, sheeby!" I called as I snuck sideways for a clear shot.

Last weekend was the opening of fishing season and the final days of the county's maple festival, so there were hundreds of city cars on the roads. Wearing gloves, I dropped the dead fox into a burlap sack while Anne built his funeral pyre. When I looked up, I saw three newish cars parked on the roadside, just watching us.

I don't know how long they'd watched and I can't guess what they thought they were seeing. Perhaps they thought we were part of the show: sheep farmers doing whatever it is sheep farmers do. As the black greasy smoke lifted, the cars all drove away. Sometimes life looks different from the other side of the safety glass.

Shearing

You might have noticed how sort of, well, *slow* most farmers move. That's because there's an infinite number of chores ahead, and if you move slowly, you get to fewer of them before you die.

Yesterday we sheared our sheep: a hundred thirty ewes, six stud rams, and a dozen ewe lambs we'll keep as replacements. For two days before shearing, we keep a close eye on the weather because rained-on wool can't be sheared. Hot dry days bring the lanolin up in the wool and make the shearing easier.

Tom Forrester always shears for us. Tom's a banty fella, a hundred fifty pounds wet, and last year he sheared twenty thousand ewes. Tom gets up at four A.M. to be down here at eight. We've got the sheep in and wool bags set up and lunch simmering on the stove for the shearing crew and a refrigerator full of Pepsi-Colas for Tom.

Tom's the gentlest shearer I know. Though sheep can be truly contrary, I've never known him to lose his temper and smack them, and he rarely cuts a ewe. The wool bags are twelve feet deep and my wife gets right inside them to stamp down the fleeces. Anne looks pretty funny with only the top of her head showing. We clip along good until noon.

Anne's fixed a nice dinner: venison stew, garden salad, stewed tomatoes, homemade bread. Tom drinks his Pepsi-Cola.

After we eat, work goes slower. The sheep seem heavier, harder to catch. My belly is full and I could use a nap.

Chi-chi-chi-chi, the clippers flash. Without their fleece, the ewes are naked, goatlike. They are opalescent against the dark green grass. They no longer recognize one another and start to butting heads. The lambs have never been sheared before and they hate it: They're ticklish.

It's six-thirty before we get to the rams. A big Rambouilette ram will weigh three hundred sixty pounds, and it takes me and Tom and Anne and my helper to get him off his feet and onto the shearing mat.

It's seven-fifteen. My back and arms are sore. The very last ram is a little smaller and I flip him by myself. "That's it," I say.

Tom grins. "Damn, I'm glad to find him. I've been looking for that last sheep all day."

Hay
Making

In the mountains it takes three days to make hay. Mow it, let it dry, rake, and bale. If it rains on mowed hay, the hay molders. If you bale the hay wet, it'll spoil, heat like a compost heap, burst into flame. Soggy, heavy hay bales are called barn burners.

Monday, when I hitched up, the mower's tires were flat. Pause while I fix them. Monday evening I had our best second-cut alfalfa knocked down.

Tuesday it clouded over and sprinkled, but no worse than the dew. It was calling for downpours on Wednesday. Our heavy rains come from the southeast, about three-thirty.

At ten Wednesday morning I was raking, rolling hay into thick windrows, when the tractor started bucking and roaring and pouring out black smoke. The drain plug had dropped out of the carburetor and all the gas was droozling out. By noon I found a bolt in the shop that more or less plugged the leak.

It was humid and hot and each bale weighed sixty pounds,

and Tom, who helps me, the heat was getting to him. About two o'clock I said I'd buck bales while Tom drove the tractor. Tom said he'd never drove a tractor. Fine, I said, this is lesson number one. He got on the seat. This gadget is the power takeoff. This lever is the hydraulics. Keep the RPM at 1620. A tractor's not like a car. When we're rolling downhill, use the gears to slow it. The brakes don't amount to much.

Three o'clock and the sky was black when Anne brought out sandwiches. She'd heard thunder, she said.

Three thirty-five. When the first drop splattered the tractor, quickly we unhitched the hay wagon, hooked it to the pickup: Go! Go! I raced the tractor, hoping to bale what was left, but fat chance. The rain came down the valley like a moving wall. Tom jammed the hay wagon in the hay field gateway and couldn't go backward or forward, so the three of us ran back to the barn for tarps.

It's hard to run lugging a droopy forty-pound tarp. That's the kind of work makes you old.

We flipped tarps over the wagon just as the heavy rain hit. Lightning electrified the woods beside the field, and we hurried back to the house hoping lightning wouldn't light us up.

It's fine hay. This winter we'll feed it to ewes with newborn lambs in pens under the barn. When I open a bale of the fragrant flowery stuff, the ewes'll bleat and baa like this bit of summer is their right. Maybe it is. Maybe it is.

Hunting

In our mountains, from October until January is hunting season. Bow season, turkey season, deer, coon, bear, small game, primitive weapons; some weeks all of the above. Fall fashions tend toward camo set off by blaze orange.

I'm of two minds about hunting. I don't hunt myself, but our farm is not posted, and last year seventeen deer were killed in our woods. I don't have a problem with that. But once the smoke settled and Anne and I started walking in the woods again, the dogs found eleven more deer carcasses. They'd been wounded somewhere else and come down to water to die. I have dreams about those deer.

In the eighteenth century, when white men settled these mountains, they killed all the competitive life: wolves, eastern mountain lion, bear, elk, deer, woods buffalo. They killed the Indians, too. By 1912, when the human population of Highland County was at its peak, deer were rare and there were no wild turkeys. Later, as marginal farms were abandoned, deer drifted back in and wild turkeys were reintroduced by the game commission. Today the deer have no natural predators. Without hunters, the deer would browse these woods bare, girdle the young trees, strip the shrubs, and ultimately starve to death. Before they died, they would graze my hay fields bare, and we and the other mountain farmers would be gone, too.

Most of the hunters I've met are decent men who save up their vacation time so they can spend a week in the woods; silent stalkers in God's creation. Sure, there are Bozos wearing blaze orange. Every year I'll see a couple carloads of Bozos cruising slowly up and down the road, rifles stuck out of every window, looking for something to kill. They don't much care what it is, either. Deer, raccoon, blacksnake, feral cat: They mean to drive the breath of life out of it.

Our city friends tend to be Bambi fans—well-meaning souls who see the deer as limpid-eyed innocents, brutalized by callous hunters. "How," they ask, "can you kill anything so beautiful?"

But all the animals we kill and eat are beautiful. Lambs are beautiful, veal calves, shy heifers, sleek sea trout, tuna, crab, deer —they are all beautiful.

Bozos and Bambi fans share a common view: Both see this countryside as Wilderness. The Bambi fans' Wilderness is romantic, filled with sweet creatures who'd do just fine if they were left alone, thank you. The Bozos' Wilderness is a dark jungle of tooth and claw where the rules of civilized conduct don't apply. Neither Bozo nor Bambi fan is willing to take the overwhelming human responsibility for animal life and death.

But there is no Wilderness. There are no wild animals. By commission or omission, all life on this planet is managed by men. We have dominion, whether we want it or not.

Blood
Money

These big purebred Suffolk rams have balls the size of apples and the seamless necks of sumo wrestlers. Black head, black legs, maybe a bit of black on the brisket or along the belly. The neck hair is curled, à la Paul Newman. They've got great long Roman noses. One expects them to shrug.

If a Rolls-Royce had a little intelligence—intelligence, say, slightly less than a dog's—one would expect the Rolls-Royce to act like these rams: certain of our admiration, certain of their place in the world.

They're big: three, three hundred fifty pounds. "I've got a thirty-three-inch inseam," Oden Thompson said, "and when I straddled Leader, I had to stand on tiptoe. His ears—they weren't too good. His ears were a little short for what I like to see."

The Fore tribe in the eastern highlands of New Guinea practices ritual cannibalism. When a kinsman dies, they eat part of him at the funeral. I don't know what reasons the Fore give for their custom. If you pause for a moment, your guesses will be much the same as mine.

Since 1957, some twenty-five hundred Fore people have died from kuru. Kuru is an invariably fatal wasting disease of the central nervous system, characterized by trembling, failure of co-ordination, dysarthria (slurred speech), dysphagia (difficulty in swallowing), and death. Kuru has killed four-year-olds and people in their sixties, but it mostly gets young adults between fifteen and thirty. When symptoms first appear, the victim has, at the outside, a year.

In 1972, in the interests of asepsis and tourism, the government of New Guinea launched a campaign to discourage canni-balism. It mostly worked. Kuru is, today, greatly reduced among the Fore people. I don't know what else happened to them.

A man just naturally wants to do better. That's why we bought Leader. We had some tremendous lambs out of him. Tremendous.

—Oden Thompson

In 1953, prompted by serious outbreaks of hoof-and-mouth disease and hog cholera, the United States Congress passed a law authorizing the Secretary of Agriculture to eradicate disease by eradicating all the animals who'd been exposed to a disease.

The law enumerated half a dozen diseases, including sheep scrapie, but the list was not meant to be exclusive. The Secretary of Agriculture has the power to kill animals exposed to *any* dis-ease "which, in the opinion of the Secretary of Agriculture, con-stitutes an emergency and threatens the livestock industry of this country."

Some months later, Secretary Ezra Taft Benson issued a di-rective on indemnification. Since public discussion of the indem-nification program would be contrary to the public interest — the Secretary said—there wouldn't be any.

The federal government pays the owners of slaughtered flocks. Up to fifty percent of their value. Under the eradication program, the feds have killed better than ninety thousand sheep. And paid up to half their value. The worst government is the government farthest from home.

Every Monday morning, quite early, Mr. Oden Thompson of Brandywine, West Virginia, drives off to work. He takes Route 33 to Elkins, catches U.S. 250 to Billington, then 92 to Morgantown, 79 over to 70 into Wheeling, and Route 7 across the bridge into Brilliant, where he's working on the new Cardinal power plant; two hundred thirty miles. He spends the week in Brilliant and comes back every weekend to his farm. In twenty years as an ironworker, this is the first job that's kept him away from home overnight. When he worked at Mount Storm, it was only a hundred eighty miles round trip, and he ate supper with his family every night.

"It's a hard, dirty, dangerous job. I ain't ever seen no easy work in ironwork."

He prefers working in the fabricating shop, welding and burning. The day goes quicker.

Oden Thompson has five sons. They're good-looking boys—a couple of them have wide-set dark eyes and this disconcertingly direct stare.

He has a hand-painted sign on his front porch:

Thompson's Wayside Rest
We cater to
hunters
fishermen
campers
deers (dears)
drunks
KIDS!

*

69

He has another, more formal sign in front of the house:

Oden Thompson & Sons
Purebred Suffolk Sheep

An orphan lamb is the perfect waif. It's January, cold and dark, and you're holding this animal in your arms because it's sick or its mother doesn't have the milk or won't own it, and the lamb is spindly-legged and still wet from the lamb bed. You put it in a box by the stove. Every winter the house smells of wood smoke and lamb piss.

Most of them die. They're very fragile. It feels as if your big clumsy hand is going to crush its rib cage.

Some survive. It's a big day when you take them outdoors into the sun for their very first lamb dance.

Scrapie is an incurable disease that will probably never be curable. Policy is eradication, not cure. It's thought that scrapie is caused by a virus, though viruses normally inflame tissue, while the scrapie virus produces a progressive degenerative disorder of the central nervous system. The scrapie virus has a remarkably long incubation period — two years plus—and is resistant to heat and chemical treatments that usually render viruses inactive.

Scrapie resembles a few other diseases, two of which occur naturally in man: kuru and Creutzfeldt-Jakob disease (C-J disease).

These diseases all *act* alike, and there's some mildly ominous research suggesting that man just *might* be susceptible to scrapie. Scrapie, kuru, and C-J disease will all "take" if inoculated into the brain of a chimpanzee. And scrapie has been transmitted from sheep to chimps and back to sheep again.

Because of the long incubation period, scrapie is a researcher's nightmare. In rare cases, scrapie has taken as long as twelve years to become active—and twelve years is very nearly a sheep's lifetime.

Scrapie is rare in the U.S., but common in England (ten thousand to fifteen thousand cases a year) and occurs throughout Europe, Asia, even Iceland. New Zealand and Australia have successfully eradicated the disease with programs very much like the U.S. program. New Zealand and Australia are islands.

If scrapie is allowed to run its course in a flock, mortality varies between two and sixty percent. It's reasonable to assume that thirty percent of an infected flock will die.

No one is quite sure how scrapie is transmitted naturally. Healthy sheep fed brain matter from infected sheep will contract the disease. But lab mice, who readily contract scrapie when inoculated, don't catch it when fed a diet of scrapie-infected urine, feces, and bedstraw.

Some researchers have claimed scrapie is transmitted genetically. There's evidence that some sheep are more susceptible to scrapie than others and, contrariwise, some may be naturally immune. Too, the disease seems to follow breeds. Some breeds, like the Dorset Down, probably never get it. Suffolks contract it readily.

The official position is that scrapie spreads from flock to flock by the movement of the infected animals who are incubating the virus. Since it's impossible to determine which sheep in an infected flock are incubating the disease, all exposed sheep are killed. In deference to the genetic theorists, the bloodline descendants of infected sheep are killed, too.

The most widely noted symptom of scrapie is the rubbing. There's debilitation, nervousness, and other signs of a nervous disorder. Finally the animal gets too weak to eat. "We'd brought Leader out from the ewes, it was the end of last October, and he was a little run down, but we thought that was from being with the ewes. He started rubbing himself on the guy line from the electric pole. We thought he might have, you know, sheep lice. He never did show any sign of nervousness except when I'd give him a shot of penicillin. He'd jump then. Oh, he could run like an elk."

Oden Thompson's a wiry man with slicked-back, gray-flecked, heavy black hair. His face gets real cheery when he talks about the kids, or lambing, or last year, when the whole family went elk hunting out West.

Here's how they handled it at lambing time. Oden Thompson would check the ewes in the morning, four or five o'clock, before he went off. One of the boys would look in at them about seven. After Jean Thompson got the kids off to school, she'd go out to the barns—usually about nine. She'd have the care of the ewes during the day. At nine-thirty that evening, Oden'd check them just before he went to bed. They didn't do any night checks. "If you get a ewe settled down at night and don't disturb her— just come in kind of quiet—they'll usually wait until morning. Then they get excited thinking about feeding, and you'll get your lambs then."

Oden Thompson paid $425 for the Leader Ram. Leader 877 was the Reserve Grand Champion—the second-place sheep of all the sheep at the Eastern Stud Ram Sale. It was the most money the Thompsons ever paid for a ram.

> That ram put us in good shape, but then he took us out.
> —Jean Thompson

A ewe died in a small West Virginia flock, and scrapie was diagnosed. The federal vets traced the disease back to the flock she'd come from as a yearling and tracked her brothers, sisters, and flockmates through flocks in Pennsylvania, Virginia, West Virginia, and New Jersey. Several bloodline sheep, including the Leader Ram, were diagnosed: scrapie. Hundreds of sheep had been exposed and were killed.

I wouldn't have wanted to be the poor SOB standing on Jean Thompson's porch, explaining that Leader 877, their ram that'd died a month ago, had probably died of scrapie, and that meant the government was going to destroy her 159 sheep, and they'd reimburse her, half the value, and she or Mr. Thompson would have to go pick up all the lambs they'd sold just last week and have them killed too, and they'd have to be buried right there on the Thompson farm; none of them could be sold for slaughter because of some cannibal disease in New Guinea.

NOTICE!

> Mr. and Mrs. Oden Thompson and sons regret to notify the public that they are no longer in the Suffolk sheep business due to the fact that a purchased stud ram whose bloodline was a suspect of scrapie (a rare and slow-acting virus), not scabie. The federal government has depopulated our flock and disposed of them on our farm.
> Thank you for your patronage in the past.
> —*Pendleton* (W. Va.) *Times*

An orphan lamb was walking around in the Thompsons' living room. Two, three weeks old, maybe a foot and a half high, maybe twenty-five pounds. Milk from its last feeding was smeared around its mouth. It was nibbling on Jean Thompson's rug.

"I guess I better take him with me," she said, and she scooped up the lamb and we drove where the flock was pastured and they were bulldozing the hole.

A terrific day. The sun had just burnt the dew off the grass, and the birds were carrying on and the occasional grumbling of a truck on the highway across the river.

The Thompsons' farm lies across the bottom of a narrow mountain valley, and the woods come down to meet the pasture on this side of the river. Yellows and greens.

There's quite a gang of us: Mrs. Thompson, her best girlfriend, Davey Thompson (age two), and a neighbor boy who's come along to help.

There's quite a gang of them: three vets, two assistants, and the dozer operator leaning against his D-6.

Oden Thompson hadn't come. He would not witness it.

The lamb is bopping along behind us, more interested in the grass than in young Davey, who's trying to play with him.

Mrs. Thompson has the kind of face that likes to laugh, and she's laughing now, though she's crying too and laughing at herself for crying.

The pit looks like the foundation for a narrow swimming pool, about eight feet deep at one end and the shallows at the other.

"We've got eighty-five big ones, and those lambs'd go a hundred pounds. How're they all going to fit in that?"

"They compact."

The vets in their coveralls and high rubber boots mixing up the curare. "It's cheaper in powder form."

Talking soft. Stringing the snow fence around the rim of the pit. The thunk of the mallet on the steel posts.

"How do they . . . they die?"

"Three to five minutes. They usually just walk off and lie down. A little muscle tremor."

Someone arriving in a pickup. "Now, you watch out! Don't you run over that lamb back there!"

And so she got the bucket and banged the handle against the side—*TAK, TAK, TAK, TAK*—and called out, "Sheeby, Sheeby, Sheeby," and the flock came out of the woods, on the run, probably thinking — like Jean Thompson said—that they were just going to get wormed.

Running, the lambs kicking up their heels, and we got behind them and swung the snow fence across the opening and closed them in. Mrs. Thompson went home. Once she'd gone, a vet picked up the orphan lamb and tossed him in with the rest. He stayed up at the shallow end near us. Like most orphan lambs, he liked people more than sheep.

And the bleats: the mothers to lambs; the lambs calling back.

They're beautiful, healthy-looking sheep. Neat, fat, their back wool slightly ridged, like corduroy, from the clippers at their last shearing.

We sort out a bunch, and Dr. Hess starts hitting them with the needle. He's got one of those automatic syringes and he jabs them in the rump, and when the needle retracts, it sounds like a zipper going up. *Zip, zip, zip,* and the birds and the distant trucks, and the sheep fold their legs under them and lie down and die.

After a while, Dr. Hess quits doing the killing. He's just getting over the flu, and he doesn't feel too good. A younger vet, Dr. Miller, who looks a little like the early James Dean in white coveralls—he takes over, *zip, zip, zip.*

There's a pretty good mound of bodies in the pit, and it's hard to walk because they shift under your feet like balloons full of bones and jelly.

And it's hot. And it's fierce. And the jokes are fierce too: "You savin' that pretty ewe for somethin'? I've got a pair of hip boots in my truck."

Swallowing noises from the dying sheep. The curare paralyzes their diaphragms. They suffocate.

"A man get hit by that needle, he wouldn't last no longer than sheep do. You don't think I'd be down here with him jabbing unless I trusted him?"

The sheep have gone quiet. Standing around, quite docile, the mothers aren't calling for their lambs anymore, and they don't go near the bodies.

"Get that ram again."

"He's had his dose. He's just chewin' on it."

When it's done, there are too many sheep in the shallow end

to be properly covered, so we throw them deeper into the pit. Some of them are very heavy and it takes two of us. The orphan lamb is light.

And the operator starts his dozer. Dr. Miller climbs out of the pit and wipes his face with the back of his hand and he's quite angry.

"It's not a very nice job," he says. "I don't care for it."

The Boys
in the
Lime-Green
Chevrolet

I'd like to speak directly to the boys in the lime-green Chevrolet, who shot two of our sheep on Monday, opening day of deer season. Shot them from the road and left them to die. Since you boys had to flee, you'd be interested to know what happened once you'd gone.

The ewes you shot had just been turned out onto pasture so they could graze; their lambs could frolic and play. When we found them, the lambs were banked up against their dead mothers. I rolled a ewe over, and when we saw the bullet hole, my wife, Anne, cried. You should understand that we're lambing and not getting much sleep and Anne's worked so hard, you see, to nurture those ewes that the thought that someone could just kill them, for the pleasure of it, for a moment—that unhinged her mind. "How could anyone do this?" she said. "What kind of person could do this?" And then she threw up.

Hunters—men—don't kill animals with young at their side. Without their mothers, young animals starve to death.

Hunters—men—know where their bullets are going. One of your bullets went through the mother and severed the lamb's leg, and the vet had to put the lamb down, she was in such pain. Of course you didn't know that. You had to flee.

You mightn't have noticed that our farm is not posted. Over the years, a good many hunters—men—have hunted deer and turkey, grouse, rabbits and squirrels here. In the years that they've been hunting, none of them has so much as left a gate open. Some of these hunters have taken supper with us. We've met their families.

I confess that my first thought when we found what you'd done was to post the farm—no hunting, no trespassing. But, you see, that would be penalizing honest men for what you did. So today we'll burn two young ewes and one lamb, and we'll try to get the lambs you orphaned on a bottle. That's harder to do than you might think.

Of course we've called the sheriff, and if you're caught, we'll prosecute. But I don't expect you'll be caught.

Two thousand years ago, Plato looked around and saw that sometimes evil-doers are not caught. Sometimes villains get away with it. Plato said the evil man has a sick soul, and every cruel, thoughtless act a man commits soils and coarsens his own soul. You killed without reason. You are less than you were.

Spare

Parts

Our station wagon turned 100,000 last week and it's the baby on the farm. The Ford flatbed we use to haul lambs to market has got 136,000 and the Dodge Power Wagon has a scant 5,000 on the odometer. Since the Power Wagon was built in 1953, I'm certain that isn't 105,000, I believe it's 205 and pray it isn't 305. Big Al, our Allis Chalmers D-17 tractor, was built in the early sixties. Most of our other farm equipment was built after the war—the second one.

Our machines are too old to be in the normal spare-parts culture. After a few years, dealers clear out their bins, throw the old service manuals away. Try going into your friendly Dodge-AMC-Mitsubishi dealer and asking for a throttle return spring for a '53 Power Wagon—the Stromberg carb, not the Carter...

Like most American farmers, we've become experts in the obsolete. We keep a drawerful of yellowing shop manuals and parts books. We keep old voltage regulators, oil seals, gaskets, carburetors. That broken transmission on the shop floor—it isn't *all* broken. First gear's still good.

Here and there, in hamlets across the United States, there are fellows who sell parts for these ancient machines. They are gurus of the Studebaker, mavens of the Minneapolis-Moline, wizards of the Edsel Ranger. These are men for whom the De Soto is not yesterday.

The Power Wagon is a brute machine, more tractor than truck. All winter we bring feed to our sheep in it. With chains on all four, there is no snowdrift it can't buck.

Last December it got to twenty below and a foot of snow, but no matter how I tapped that ammeter gauge on the old Dodge, it wouldn't budge. The generator was shot. One of the things about sheep is their indifference to the shepherd's troubles. Every day, they need to eat.

Christmas Eve I phoned Dave Butler out in Fairfield, Iowa, and the day after Christmas the generator got here. The 1950s was the heyday for American machines and they sure knew how to pack a spare part. Unwrapping the generator was like unwrapping a time capsule. First I pried apart the sturdy wooden crate. Then I removed the silica bags put in there in case the part was sent to the jungle and needed to be kept dry. Finally, I unwrapped the heavy, cosmolined wrapping paper around the spanking new green Dodge generator that had been placed in that box thirty-six years ago by a Detroit auto worker long since retired.

It was a funny sort of Christmas miracle.

Life in the
Fast Lane

February is the longest month of the year. The old snow on our farm has changed to slush and gray ice and mud that can suck a rubber boot right off your foot. Whenever there's fresh snow, our dirt road is nearly impassable, and we ferry feed and groceries in our ancient four-wheel-drive pickup. With so many lambs on the ground, feeding gets complicated and the free time between morning and evening chores gets short. We've been lambing since December, and the marvel of new birth has become another routine job.

In the fall, we can take real pleasure in a full freezer, neat woodpiles, the barn groaning with hay. We look forward to quiet winter evenings—reading beside the fire, doing a jigsaw puzzle, perhaps hooking a new rug for the living room. But by February we've done those things, and the prospect of one more quiet country evening can set my teeth on edge.

That's when city life looks good. Anne and I imagine ourselves eating out in a nice little restaurant with wine and candlelight. We want to see a movie on a screen bigger than nineteen inches, measured diagonally. We dream about concerts, ballet, gallery openings, dancing. We long for what Anne calls "life in the fast lane."

Harrisonburg, our shopping town, is only forty miles away, but bad roads and mountains make for a slow trip: an hour and a half one way. When lambs are coming, we rarely go there together, but this particular morning we decided to chance it. The two ewes, we'd been expecting to lamb did so, considerately, at six-thirty A.M. A good single, and twins. Most of our ewes twin, some single, and occasionally a ewe will drop triplets.

The ewe due to lamb next was Bouncer, a big young Rambouillet who had proved her mothering ability the past year. She wasn't pawing herself a nest, or walking aimlessly about, or licking her lips, or separating herself from the flock. A neighbor promised to check Bouncer at noon, so we took off.

The trip in was pleasant; we made good time and stopped for chili dogs at Jess's Quick Lunch, not exactly the candlelit restaurant I had dreamed about.

We had a noontime appointment with our income-tax preparer. Mrs. Peters is very sharp, but new to the area and to farm accounting. When we sat down, I was nervous, expecting the worst possible news. I chattered about the weather, which was supposed to turn cold and windy.

She asked if we had more lambs when the weather changed. She had been talking to a dairy farmer who always got his calves during sudden cold snaps. He claimed stress brought on labor.

I said, "That hasn't been our experience. Oh, when the weather's very bad, we check the ewes every couple of hours because newborn lambs are so fragile. When it's below zero, if a newborn isn't up and nursing within twenty minutes, he'll freeze to death. But I haven't noticed more lambs coming during bad weather."

Anne thought the dairy farmer was probably right. "It makes sense to me. Stress can start the contractions."

Pleasantries concluded, Mrs. Peters gave us the news about our taxes. It wasn't as bad as I had feared. So I was in a pretty good mood as we did our shopping. We picked up groceries, milk replacer (for orphan lambs), and an order of vet supplies for a neighbor. Outside the Farmer's Co-op, I eyed a display of fruit trees: apple, pear, peach, and cherry trees with green plastic wrapped around their root balls. I'd been meaning to plant an orchard for years. Maybe this year . . .

It started to get colder as the truck ground up the steep curves of Shenandoah Mountain, but the scudding clouds overhead didn't look like snow. As soon as we got home, I checked the lambing yard. Bouncer stared at me placidly, a wisp of hay hanging out of her mouth.

I said, "Bouncer, you should probably go right ahead and lamb. You'll like it inside the barn. Besides, ewes with lambs eat better."

Bouncer didn't comment; she stuck her head back into the hay feeder.

The dozen ewes in the lambing yard were older commercial sheep. Some were Rambouillets (white-faced, long-wooled ewes), some had the black head and short fleece of the Suffolk breed, and some were crossbreeds with dusky, speckled faces. They were big ewes—a hundred fifty to a hundred eighty pounds—and all of them were experienced mothers.

We unloaded our provisions and started feeding the different groups of sheep. In the west, the sky was a pale, brilliant blue. The wind was starting to come up. I hauled water to the barn for the ewes with lambs and quickly checked all the lambs for health by sticking a finger in their mouths. If a lamb is healthy and nursing, the mouth is warm. But if a lamb's mouth is cold, you had better do something right away.

We feed hay off the back of a two-wheeled cart. As soon as I broke a bale open, the wind rolled and scattered it. It was work to pull the big field gates closed, but even when Anne said she had tied the barn doors with baling twine because of the wind, I didn't worry. Our farm lies across the bottom of a long, narrow valley. It's a natural wind tunnel and we've had high winds before. You get used to the tin roof shaking and rattling and the creak of house timbers.

The thermometer outside stood at ten degrees. No big deal.

I poured myself a cup of coffee and sat down to watch Walter Cronkite. Anne pulled off her high rubber boots and put on her slippers.

"The sheep hate that wind," she said. "Did you see how spooked the ewes were?"

The forecast was for gusts up to fifty mph, but I pushed more wood into the stove and the house was very warm.

"I'll do the dishes if you cook," I suggested.

"Fair enough."

It was a good dinner, too: pepper steak, baked potatoes, and peas. The howling outside made the house seem especially snug, and we settled in for a quiet evening. Anne had her feet up, waiting for her favorite TV program, "M*A*S*H," which came on at eight-thirty.

"I'm going to take a bath," I said. "I'll do a quick sheep check before I get in the tub."

"If you want to. I checked an hour ago and nobody was doing anything. Bouncer will probably wait until morning."

"Yeah, well . . ."

I put on my down vest and windbreaker and took the heavy sealed-beam flashlight. The lambing yard is only twenty feet from the house, and I had just stepped outside when I heard the familiar nicker of a ewe to her newborn lamb. It's a lovely sound, a soft *uh-uh-uh,* and it made me smile. I thought, Well, we're not done for the night after all.

As soon as I opened the lambing-yard gate, I spotted her. The frantic mother, a big Suffolk, was trying to rouse her lambs —she'd had triplets—but they were all flat on the ground, motionless as boards. I ran back to the house and shouted, "Anne! Come quick!"

The ewe had done her best: She had cleaned each lamb as it came, and had tried to nudge them to their feet, but they were down now—muddy, bloody, and stiff. I wiped the birth mucus off their faces and forced by finger into their mouths. Cold. Ice cold. One lamb's ribs heaved with breath, and he was using his last strength to lift his heavy head a few inches off the ground.

Anne was beside me now. We scooped up the filthy, frozen lambs in our arms, hurried back to the house, and laid them beside the wood stove, just six inches from the hot metal.

"Quick," Anne snapped, "get some warm water in the sink. Don't make it too hot." She was slapping at their sides, rubbing them down with a lambing towel. It looks a little rough, but you have to get the circulation going.

For triplets, they were very big: close to ten pounds each. Since multiple births are hereditary in sheep, these were very special lambs.

Anne was drawing medicine into a syringe as I plunged the worst lamb into the warm water. Its long, floppy ears were frozen into wings and I was afraid I might break them. When the lamb touched the water, it turned black and slimy. Anne was talking to the others as she injected them with AA1000 (a mixture of B vitamins, glucose, and electrolytes). As she slid the needle into their icy flanks, she was crooning, "Come on, honey. You can live. You can breathe now. *Hey, this one is breathing!*" And she brought both her lambs to the double sink. I was trying to fill the other side but couldn't find the stopper, and the warm water cascaded down my lamb's sides. Its eyes were half open, but slowly its eyelids slid closed.

"Quick. I'll give this one a hit." Anne's deft hands slipped the needle into the folds of loose skin over the ribs.

"I'm giving her three cc's," she said. "Is it a her?"

"I haven't looked. Yes. I can't use this sink."

"Use the sink in the bathroom."

The lamb overflowed the shallow basin of the bathroom sink. I cradled her head just above the filthy water and splashed water on her fine pointy nose to dissolve the strands of frozen mucus still clinging there. I held her up to my ear. Her eyes were closed and she wasn't breathing, but something tapped faintly inside the chest cavity.

"I'm done in here!" Anne called. She swept into the living room with two thoroughly drenched lambs and an armload of the towels we use for lambing.

"I've got to try mouth-to-mouth," I said as I moved back to the deep sink again.

A lamb's muzzle will fit completely into a human mouth, so you can blow into the nostrils and mouth at the same time. Holding the lamb in the water, I enclosed its muzzle and puffed, took a breath, pressed its rib cage for the exhale, and puffed again. A lamb's lungs are smaller than a human baby's. It doesn't take much air to fill them. Gently, gently. Puff, breathe, press, puff, breathe, press. The lamb's muzzle was still icy cold. The air from her lungs tasted strange but clean in my mouth.

The warm water had brought my lamb's body temperature up, but she wasn't breathing on her own. Anne came in and added more hot water. "How is she?"

When I drew back, the tiny mouth opened. The bright red tongue came out a quarter-inch and retracted. "Can't tell. Either she's got some spark still left in her, or she's started her death spasms."

Puff, breathe, press, puff, breathe. No obstructions in her air passages, and it didn't feel as if I was pushing air into her stomach.

When I pulled her out of the water, her eyes stayed closed,

she was totally limp, but her sides heaved convulsively, once, twice. She settled into a regular breathing pattern. "Hey! All right!" I yelled, and carried her to lie on the towel beside her brothers. Two wet ram lambs and one wet ewe lamb. Anne and I knelt side by side, rubbing life into the newborn. Both of us were nattering heedlessly.

"Their mother can't raise triplets," Anne said.

"Why not? She's a big ewe."

"She had mastitis last year. She's got only one teat."

The two ram lambs were wriggling around, trying to sit up straight. The ewe lamb lay still. I slapped her face, rubbed briskly, and promised her the sun, moon, stars, and a good mother if she'd just open her eyes.

"I'll bet their mother is going bananas," Anne said. I pictured the mother, bleating and tearing around the yard searching for her missing babies. But when I stepped into the yard, I couldn't hear the ewe. Some sheep were peacefully pulling hay out of the feeder. A mother was nickering to a newborn.

Very quickly, I understood why the Suffolk wasn't hysterical about her lost lambs. She had found another one. That it wasn't hers didn't matter. I found two ewes nickering and nuzzling a big white single lamb who was sitting up comfortably, receiving the attentions of two mothers' tongues. When I checked the lamb's mouth, it was warm. He was in the lee of the feeder and the wind wasn't getting to him.

As I came through the kitchen, I said, "We've got another one. We can put him on hold for a while."

Anne had one lamb in her lap, trying it with a bottle. She had heated a mixture of colostrum and milk replacer, and was nudging the lamb's lips with the bottle.

My weak ewe lamb had her eyes open. I christened her "Lazarus."

Anne went outside and brought the other newborn back with her. When I'd seen him, he'd been as clean and white as a pearl.

Now he was muddy, gasping, and half frozen. We got a fresh towel and went to work. Apparently, one of his "mothers" had got him up to nurse, but when he wobbled away from the windbreak, the wind had dropped him like a stone.

"He's big."

"Must go fifteen pounds."

One white lamb and three blackfaces, side by side on a crimson towel. Anne was working all of them, teaching them how to nurse. When a weak lamb first finds its suck, it's as though an electric shock passes through it. One can almost hear the lamb say "Aha! So that's the idea." And it changes from a fumbling, passive creature to support the primary urge: *more milk!*

As they began to stand, we moved them into the front room, where the rug gave them better footing. They stumbled around, bleating and searching the corners. When they ran into one another, they would drop to their knees and try to nurse one another's ears. By ten-thirty, we had one lamb tangled in the fireplace screen, another trying to nibble a lamp cord, and enough noise for a zoo. Big White had a tremendous *baa,* Lazarus a squeaky bleat.

It's always chancy pulling brand-new lambs off their mothers. The bonding process, in which the mother recognizes the lamb as her own, is fairly delicate, and sometimes, when the process is disturbed, the ewe will refuse a lamb and let it starve or even butt it to death in the lambing pen. You can raise lambs on bottles, but they never do as well as lambs raised by a good mother.

Ewes recognize their lambs by scent, but we had washed all the scent off the triplets. Anne eyed the clumsy, healthy lambs. "Fine," she said. "Now we have four lambs and two mothers that both want the big white one."

We would have to try and graft one of the triplets onto Big White's mother. The Suffolk could raise two lambs on one teat. Perhaps the ewes were so confused by now that they wouldn't know one lamb from another.

By eleven-thirty, the lambs were strong enough to go outside.

The wind had died down. We each carried two lambs. As soon as the ewes heard them, they went crazy, calling for the lambs, rushing back and forth. They were like woolly gunboats circling us, trying to get to the lambs, and when we stepped into the barn, all the other ewes, suddenly awakened and alarmed, started calling for their lambs. We laid the lambs in the straw of the lambing pens. The lambs found it hard to walk in the deep straw and weren't too certain of their direction, but they were in fine voice. The ewes fell silent. Reserving judgment, they extended their noses to sniff the lambs. With a soft nicker and swipe of her rough tongue, the Suffolk owned two lambs and resumed the job that had been so rudely interrupted. Big White's mother welcomed him right away but sniffed the grafted newcomer suspiciously. You could practically see her thinking, Two lambs? But I'm almost sure I had only one lamb. Almost sure . . . Then Lazarus let out a particularly lusty cry and the ewe accepted the stranger and nudged her back toward her milk.

When Anne checked at one A.M., the lambs on the Suffolk had learned to take turns on her one functional teat.

When I went out at three, all four lambs were asleep, banked up against their mothers. There's nothing so smug as a lamb with a full belly. When I put my finger in Lazarus's mouth, she bleated in outrage.

When Anne went out at five, all the lambs were fine and Bouncer promptly presented her with two new ones. An effortless, routine delivery. Bouncer's lambs were up and nursing while she was still cleaning them off.

Later, over breakfast, Anne laughed. "Life in the fast lane," she said.

Snowbound

We are snowbound. There's eight inches on the ground, and Shenandoah Mountain, its ridges and hollows, are pen and ink sketches, fading in and out of the falling snow. Our dirt road has twelve families in as many miles and is the last road the snowplows get to. The snowplows are busy with the big highways, the interstates, helping people who have some-place to go.

We are going no place. This morning I counted the hay in the old barn. The center bay is empty, but both side bays are a solid mass of bales—two thousand, I figure. In July and August it was real work bucking those bales into the loft, the hay chaff sticking to my sweat and the dust making me sneeze. But now each leafy green bale is pure pleasure to the ewes when we spread it out on top of the snow.

Whenever it gets like this, feeding gets heavier because the sheep can't paw through the snow to the grass underneath and we've got three separate flocks plus the rams, and by the time we're done, the sheep dogs are wet and happy and snug up next to the stove, so we have to step over them when we want to dry our boots.

There's plenty of work to do outside, I know. But I'm not going to do it. We're snowbound. I've got Jim Harrison's new book and I'll read that instead.

The freezer's full of vegetables, lamb, and deer meat. There's a hundred quarts of tomatoes in the root cellar, fifty quarts of beans.

Last February, I cut and stacked our firewood so it dried all summer. There's a cord on the porch and another four cords just outside covered with black plastic. It's true what they say: Firewood warms you three times—once when you cut it, once when you split it, but the best time is when you're inside and your boots are sizzling by the fire, and Anne is baking bread and you're snowbound.

The

Christmas

Lamb

We don't pay too much mind to Christmas, here on the farm. We've got a couple hundred sheep to feed and chores take two or three hours, morning and evening. It gets dark too early.

We cut a cedar for a Christmas tree. Cedars don't make very good Christmas trees, but we've got a lot of them. Some country folks decorate their mailboxes with lights and holly, but we don't bother.

Last year, the day before Christmas was twenty below. Even with chains on all four wheels of the old Power Wagon, it was hard bucking through the drifts. Dry ewes can get enough liquid eating snow, but our ewes are milking with lambs on them and need fresh water, so after morning chores (by then it was noon), I walked down to the pond and busted a hole in the six-inch ice.

The snow had collapsed an old maple tree, so I spent the afternoon cutting firewood.

Evening chores, a bitter wind came up, so we put out feed as quickly as we could and started back for the house. I saw something fluttering down at the hole in the pond. My heart sank. I hoped it was just a bird, drinking.

What I'd seen was a lamb's ears. He'd skidded into the icy, chunky water and couldn't pull himself back out. I dragged him by one leg and pressed him to my ear and heard . . . heartbeat. I ran back to the house with him tucked under my arm like a forty-pound frozen plank. Bang into the house, "Anne!" into the bathroom, dropped him into the tub, and started running hot water. "Not too hot," Anne commanded. I held his head out of the water, swirling warmth over his wool.

Kneeling by the tub, soaked to the elbows, I worked at it for five minutes before he warmed up enough to breathe.

We dried him off and swaddled him in sheepskins before the fire, and the dogs came over and took one look and disapproved. Sheep dogs are very conservative and don't like to see lambs in the house. Wrapped in sheepskins, he looked like a woolly eggroll. We put the bundle into a dog kennel beside the fire where he could sleep.

Since it was Christmas Eve, we put on clean clothes and drove down to Windy Cove Church, where they always have a candlelight service.

There's an old story that, on Christmas Eve, all the farm animals are allowed to talk. That night they praise the Christ child and remember the manger, the stall, in which he lay.

We were in church at midnight, so I don't know whether that lamb talked, resting there in the darkened house, beside the crackling fire.

At Windy Cove Church, a choir of country kids in clean blue jeans and clip-on bow ties sang: "The first Noel, the angels did say, was to certain poor shepherds in fields as they lay. In fields where they lay keeping their sheep, on a cold winter's night that was so deep."

PART III

The
Animals

Starting
Out with
Stock
Dogs

A good stock dog can replace three men loading hogs, will fetch your milk cows morning and evening, can pluck goats out of the thicket and sort sheep. Stock dogs improve your poor fences, substitute for good handling facilities, and stabilize your blood pressure when your deaf neighbor's forty cows have busted through the water gate again and are standing in your newly planted alfalfa, chowing down.

A badly handled stock dog is a nuisance on the farm.

Very badly handled, stock dogs can get themselves in awful trouble.

If this were Scotland, you could just go down the road, buy a dog, and learn from a neighbor how to work it, but there is no tradition for handling working dogs in the United States, and the common store of dog knowledge is nearly worthless.

A stock dog is not a pet. Pets require human praise for their self-esteem. A stock dog's sense of worth comes from properly accomplishing the tasks set for it. Stock dogs can be companions or coworkers or fellow travelers on the karmic wheel, but they are not pets. Most of them aren't pretty, either.

Don't buy a stock dog if you have a houseful of other dogs. You and your stock dog will both spend too much time relating to the other dogs.

Don't buy more than one stock dog. If you buy a bitch, don't breed her and keep a pup. Professional trainers can handle six or eight dogs at one time. Two's my limit. Start with one.

In the past, there were a great many herding breeds. Most of those breeds have had their stock instincts bred out of them to become attractive pets. It's a shame. The English Sheepdog is a pet. The Puli is a pet. The Shelty is a pet. The Standard Collie (the Lassie Collie) first attracted attention in the 1870s when Queen Victoria imported them from Balmoral, Scotland, to London. Standard Collies became the rage. Particularly handsome animals changed hands for big money. One day a group of fanciers decided to hold a trial for their beautiful animals. They located an estate and chartered a train for themselves, their guests, and their dogs. The affair attracted considerable attention and excited the press. Members of the royal family (though not the queen) were in attendance.

They laid out a trial course modeled after the course that the rougher, plebeian Border Collies ran.

Manicured, groomed, gorgeously colored Standard Collies were assembled on a lush lawn. A hundred and fifty yards away, workmen released some sheep. For weeks afterward, men still searched for those sheep, which the dogs had scattered halfway across the county. To my knowledge, that was the one and only time Standard Collies ever worked livestock.

The Welsh Collie, Bearded Collie, and Corgi (Pembroke variety) are sometimes found working stock in England. In this country, the Australian Shepherd and Catahoulus are used as cow dogs in the West. Some stock men swear by them, particularly for close work with rough animals. They're relatively heat-tolerant.

I've only seen one Australian Kelpie, and it worked much like a Border Collie.

If you fancy one of these breeds, go ahead. There's no arguing with the heart. Be sure to buy from a breeder who has working (not show) stock, and pick a breeder who will help you out when you have questions or difficulties.

For twenty-three years, sheep dog trials have been held in Lexington, Kentucky. The Bluegrass Open Sheep Dog Trials are the Kentucky Derby of sheep-dog events, the most important trials in the country. There, dogs are sent out three hundred yards to gather five Texas yearling ewes that have never been worked by a dog before. The sheep are wild—extremely spooky. (As one old handler put it, "Last time those sheep saw a dog, it was eating their mama.") Obedient to voice and whistle commands, the stock dog must bring these difficult sheep to the handler's feet, then drive them one hundred yards away through a narrow gate, cross-drive the field through another gate, and return them to the handler's feet, where man and dog attempt to force them into a six-by-eight-foot pen. After the penning, the sheep are released, and the dog must shed off the two with red ribbons around their necks.

The Bluegrass Open Sheep Dog Trials are a grueling test of a dog. In twenty-three years only one non–Border Collie has entered the Bluegrass, and it never qualified for the finals. Most novice stock-dog handlers would be best off buying a Border Collie. There's a good working stock in this country and, as with Ford and Chevrolet, plenty of dealers.

If you don't wish to train your own dog, you can buy a started dog, a "made" (completely trained) dog, or you can engage a professional trainer. Most of the made dogs you can buy are imported from Scotland, some from England or Wales.

Border Collies work from about eighteen months to ten years of age. A trained dog's price will depend on age and prospects. A dog that is a real trial contender in Scotland will cost you much more than a workaday farm dog. I've heard of imported trial dogs fetching nearly ten thousand dollars. Of course, most are more modest in price. I know a Virginia farmer who routinely imports older farm dogs for about eight hundred dollars each. Plus air fare: That's another four hundred.

Naturally, the Scots don't wish to export their best dogs; they prefer to keep them for trials, stud, and breeding. Scots aren't daft. But many excellent dogs have been shipped to the United States —as well as a few bum ones. If you import directly from Scotland, you can expect to get a cassette tape of commands and whistle signals you must learn perfectly. They are the only language your dog understands.

Many American breeders have a few imported dogs for sale. Either the dogs have grown too old to win trials, or they didn't turn out, or sometimes the breeder simply can't get along with them. Some of these breeders will have domestically trained dogs for sale, too; generally—though not always—these are dogs they have trained themselves. A started dog (a dog that knows its left and right, can fetch sheep and hold them up to you) will cost a thousand dollars. If you like the dog, this can be a hell of a buy. A fully trained dog that can fetch, drive, cross-drive, and pen to voice or whistle commands will cost thirty-five hundred dollars or more.

Puppies are not expensive—between one hundred fifty and four hundred dollars should do it. If you send your dog off for professional training, expect to pay from two hundred to three hundred a month.

Your breeder should guarantee his pups to work. If, by the age of eighteen months, your pup has never shown interest in livestock, you should be able to return him for the puppy price.

Most breeders will be happy to brag about your pup's's lineage, which should impress you little. Almost all the registered pups in this country are well bred. Almost all of them can claim some Wiston Cap in the bloodline or Gilchrist Spot or McTeir's

Ben. You *should* be particular about working parents. If possible, arrange to see the dam work before the pups are born. The breeder might not run her when she's run down from whelping. If the sire is on premises, watch him, too. If you don't like both sire and dam, do not buy a pup.

Your dog will be registered with the International Sheep Dog Society, the North American Sheep Dog Society, the International-American Sheep Dog Registry, or the American Border Collie Association. Professional sheep-dog people can get real hot about the virtues and vices of the various registries, but these internal disputes needn't concern you. Each of the registries accepts the other's registrations, and all draw on the same gene pool. For the beginner's purposes, they are interchangeable.

Border Collies are not recognized by the American Kennel Club and cannot be shown in the breed ring. They are not bred for conformation, to breed type, or for beauty. Good worker is bred to good worker. Thus, bad Border Collies are rare. Bad handlers are common as dirt.

If you're lucky, the man who sells you your dog will be concerned that your dog work out. He'll give you advice, answer those late-night telephone questions, and sometimes let you bring your dog back to his place for a training session or two. If you're unlucky, the breeder won't give you the time of day after your check has cleared. If you don't know dogs, you ought to know men.

Many reputable breeders advertise in the sheep journals, but you'd be wise to meet your breeder face to face. Dog trials are held across the country from spring to late fall. Most of them are sheep trials, but there are cattle and hog trials as well. At these trials, there's a certain amount of dog trading, and no doubt somebody will have a box of puppies for sale.

Watch the Open Class dogs run. Any dog good enough to run in the Open Class would make an excellent farm dog, and any man who can handle such a dog can teach you a thing or two. Pay special attention to handling style. Winners come and go, but a handling style that suits you might be yours always. Buy your dog from someone you can emulate. If you have cows or hogs, buy from a breeder experienced with these animals. Cow-and-hog dog training is somewhat specialized, and in general, these dogs must be more powerful and aggressive than dogs used only on sheep.

Whether you buy a trained dog or a pup, you will need to ask your dog to work for you. You must convince him that you are a wise leader, especially knowledgeable in the ways of live-stock. You will need to know more than he does.

Bring the dog into the house. I don't give a damn for any man who expects his dog to work his heart out but won't allow him into his home. Give the dog a pad or folded blanket some-where out of the way. It's not hard to keep a dog off the furniture.

If you've got kids, they'll socialize the dog. If not, trail your dog about. When you're not doing machine work, take him with you to the fields. If it isn't too hot, take him into town. Train him to ride on the passenger floorboards, and he won't get your seats muddy, plus he'll stand a better chance of surviving an accident. Take him around, on lead, and introduce him. Teach him the world you want him to know.

Keep your hands to yourself. If beatings made good dogs, there'd be millions of good dogs. Generally, when a stock dog misbehaves, he's overexcited, confused, afraid, or ignorant of what you want. Rarely, a dog is hardheaded and thinks he's top dog. If such a dog persists in willful misbehavior, take him by the ruff, lift it, glare in his eyes, and give him a shake.

We feed our dogs a good high-protein dry dog food. When they're working hard, competing at trails, or slogging through mud and snow, we supplement the diet with meat.

Those who hunt or butcher at home will have scraps to feed and freeze. Those who do not should buy canned dog meat like Alpo. Read the labels. Avoid soybean meal, unpronounceable fla-vorings, and preservatives. Cull ewes that bring fifteen dollars at the livestock market would probably serve better butchered and ground into meat for the dogs.

Your dog has highly developed herding instincts. He may well wish to herd cars, tractors, and trucks. I know few professional handlers who haven't lost dogs to cars. Some handlers recommend you keep your dog chained unless he's working or exercising. I don't ever let our dogs follow vehicles or greet cars when they arrive at our farm. When walking the dogs down our dirt road, I lie them down when a vehicle passes. I trust that frequently worked dogs won't develop bad habits, and so far, so good.

Stock dogs are not thrifty keepers. Any dog that routinely jumps barbed-wire fences is bound to get hung up now and again. We seem to average one emergency call per dog per year, and the vet bills add up. Shots, worming, heartworm medication, and emergency calls run around two hundred fifty dollars per dog per annum. Be sure you've located a good small-animal vet you can reach on Sundays and holidays.

Border Collies are dark-coated, cool-climate dogs, and it is quite possible to work them to death. Like all dogs, they "sweat" only through their tongues and the pads of their feet. Overworked or overheated, they can be poisoned by an inability to remove their own body wastes.

Last July, one of our ewes escaped into the pasture next door, where she joined a flock of fifty sheep and as many Simmental cattle. Although the temperature was in the nineties, I took our older dog, Pip, and a six-month-old puppy to get the ewe back. I chained the pup, and Pip went to work, shedding off cattle ten at a time and then shedding off sheep. An hour later, Pip had reduced the flock to just three (our ewe and an extra ewe and lamb), and he was pretty near done. He'd stand at my command and try, but his hindquarters shook and he collapsed whenever I gave him a "Lie down." Our gate was open. The ewe was so close. Just a few more minutes. Each time I asked Pip, he got up and gave it another try, though his tongue hung out a yard and his eyes were glazing. Finally, I sent the puppy in to help. The pup knew we were in trouble. Working together, the barely trained strong pup and the failing older dog brought our ewe home. I looked into Pip's eyes and felt bad. The nearest water was a cattle tank, a half-mile away. With Pip in my arms, I ran. I immersed him in the tank and cooled him until he was able to stand again, trembling. I carried him home. Three days later he was able to work again. Even fools have good luck sometimes.

Whether you intend to train your own dog or buy one trained, you will need to become a capable handler. A neighbor once bought a twelve-hundred-dollar cattle-and-sheep dog, complete with a cassette of whistle commands. The neighbor could scarcely blow the shepherd's whistle (there's a knack to it) and was unable to imitate the commands. The dog was hardheaded, the breeder unreachable for advice. One afternoon, I watched my neighbor send his dog after a distant flock of sheep. As the dog made his gather, a car arrived full of friends. With some relief, my neighbor quit his futile whistling and went to greet the newcomers, abandoning the dog to whatever he wanted to do—which was chase sheep and bite their hocks. Soon the dog was quite useless and spent most of the remainder of his life chained, until he got loose long enough to be run down by a car.

Although not particularly time-consuming, training a stock dog takes know-how, attentiveness, and some slight gift with animals. I shan't offer any training tips in this short space. You can learn to train and handle a dog through apprenticeship, reading, or—in my view the easiest way—by signing up with a stock-dog handler's clinic. Every year, there are several dozen of these clinics in the United States and Canada. Most are two- or three-day affairs. At the clinic, novices get the chance to work their dogs under the eye and guidance of a man who has spent years working stock dogs. Clinics can be extremely useful. They cost about seventy dollars per dog per day, plus what you spend on food, motels, and travel.

I've emphasized the difficulties and responsibilities of owning a stock dog. If you do your part of the job, likely your dog will do his. Working a good dog can be lovely: a real connection with an alien mind. One December evening you'll go out to bring in the bred ewes, and it'll be driving snow, and those hummocks way at the far end of the pasture might be sheep and might not, too, and the light will be failing. Quietly, you'll send your dog into the dusk, where his knowledge and heart will bring your sheep safely home. That's why stock dogs have one-syllable names: Ben, Nell, Pip, Lass, Cap, Hope. You can cry their names into the teeth of the wind.

Rose

We took Rose because a bad man hankered after her and was making vague and interesting threats. Rose lived in West Virginia on a mountain farm with spectacular views and no good road to speak of. It was dusk in the spring of the year when we walked in there. Rose was two years old, fresh off her first calf, a "Ladybroke" Guernsey, and Anne and I and Carol (our resident cow expert) looked her over. "She has nice teats," Carol said. We agreed that she did. "And a nice tight udder." We didn't like a huge bag either. In the moonlight, I led Rose down the trail wondering what in the world I'd do if she decided to make a run for it. But even when we had to ford a knee-deep ice-cold mountain river, she came along quietly.

During the first week we milked in shifts. Anne would milk and I'd take over when she just couldn't stand it anymore. Those milkings took us about an hour.

There's a knack to milking a cow. She's got to let down her milk and she won't do that unless she's feeling agreeable. So Anne and I sang to her. We sang "Second-Hand Rose." We sang "Old Brown Rosie." We sang "The Rose of Tralee."

Her foamy milk filled the bucket two gallons at a time. That's considerable milk and butter and cream too thick to pour. At first, we tried raising hogs on the extra, but that didn't work out so well. When the sows came into heat, they'd escape from our pen and scoot under the house, and I'd have to crawl under there after the huge amorous beasts.

Finally, we just let Rose keep her calves. The calf would milk one side and we'd milk the other. That worked out better.

There is something soothing about leaning your weary head into a cow's yeasty flank and milking her, *jit, jit, jit, jit.* I came to enjoy it.

We had Rosie for ten years. She started coming down with milk fever whenever she calved, and finally she aborted a calf and then she wouldn't catch at all. She'd come into season but we couldn't get her settled. I thought to send Rose to market, but Anne said, "Nobody sells their milk cow." I guess you don't. We put Rose out to pasture.

A couple years back, a flood came down our valley and took out all the fences. Instead of being five adjacent farms, we became one continuous farm, and animals drifted from one homestead to another. The flood had put us all in a state of shock and it was several days before I wondered: Where was Rosie? I found her on a neighbor's farm. Seems she'd come into season and decided to visit the neighbor's bull, and she'd got herself stuck in a quagmire and had a heart attack trying to get out.

On spring days sometimes when I came out to milk Rosie, she'd go galloping off down the field, her bag flying from side to side, buckling and dancing like a silly calf. That was Rosie's idea of a joke.

Old Brown Rosie, the Rose of Alabama. My sweet Terbaccy Posie is the Rose of Alabama. . . .

Dog Hunting

The little black dog was lousy, pot-bellied from worms. She'd been abused—you could tell by the way she showed us kids sneaky teeth. But me and my little sister Carol had brought her off the street and oh, how we wanted to keep her. If she hadn't bit Carol, I think our parents would have gone along with our plan. As my father took the dog out of the car, I cried, "Dad, don't take her to the pound! Take her out to the country and turn her loose. She'll be okay in the country, Dad!"

When my father came home, I never asked what he'd done with her. Even at nine years old, there are things you don't want to know.

Forty years later, I live in the country and raise sheep and I feel differently about family pets dropped off in the country by owners too tender-hearted to have them put down. I won't describe what happens when dogs get into a flock of sheep. I will say the carnage can leave a grown man sick and trembling.

It's not legal to shoot the thoughtless humans who pause on some country road, jerk off Rover's collar, and push him out of the car. When you catch Rover in the midst of your sheep, it is legal to shoot Rover.

The people who leave a family pet trotting behind their escaping car are not nine years old. Just what do they think the dog is going to eat?

Every couple years, stray dogs form a dog pack and start marauding in our valley. The farmers load the rifles they keep in their pickup racks and stay up very late at night and sleep light.

Normally, when dogs get in the flock, they'll run them to hell and gone and, next day, the survivors are so spooked you can't get near them. This time was different. When we got hit, only one ewe was killed, just her liver eaten and all her mates grazing peacefully around her.

It was a full moon, so I opened the barn's loft doors, pulled hay bales into a bed, laid my thermos and rifle next to me, and my dog Rusty, too. It was Rusty's job to nudge me awake when something came.

I'd wake at two or three A.M., above a ghost landscape. Rifle scopes gather light, so I'd scope that twenty-acre field, every dark shadow, every bush shape I hadn't remembered from the night before. Rusty would nuzzle me. I'd take a drink from my thermos.

Scent rises and I was above the ewe's scent line, but somehow they knew I was there and, after the third night, always bedded down under the lee of the barn. They were seeking a shepherd's protection.

Although I slept in that barn until the moon got too small to shoot by its light, I never did see anything. What I remember is how peaceful it was, how beautiful.

Our neighbor Glavis Alt killed the beast who had been taking so many sheep and it turned out to be a coyote. He'd killed sixty sheep in all. God, he was a handsome brute: powerful chest, muscular hindquarters, stiff reddish fur.

When he was dead, all the farmers relaxed. I was kind of glad he wasn't a dog.

Granma

We don't name our ewes. They all have ear tags with numbers. As Anne says, when you load lambs for market, you don't want them following you onto the truck.

When Granma first got here, she was eleven years old. Two farmers down the road, Chief and Lewis Hupman, had raised her as a pet lamb and Granma followed them everywhere. "She's a good mother. Couldn't be better."

Of course, they couldn't bear to send the old girl to slaughter, and we were new enough in the business to take her. Eleven years is an old, old sheep.

We didn't have any pens or fences, so we brought her into the front yard when she started to lamb. She dropped her first waterbag and we ran for the vet books. The book said we should wait an hour or so after she started laboring before we got worried. We waited. Waited a little longer. Granma groaned and heaved.

Once you get hold of the lamb's feet, the ewe won't try to escape, and an hour and a half after Granma started, that's all she had out, one foot. I scrubbed my hands and went inside, past the cervix (it's so narrow it hurts your hand) and into the birth canal, where I found an enormous head. I pushed it back to get room, plucked the other leg by, and got the other foot out. And that's as far as I got. Two feet and a nose tip and tongue. I couldn't pull that lamb out.

Our neighbor Ancel Luxford had more experience than we did and he came down when we phoned. For another half hour, he tried, too, every trick he knew, but the lamb was just too big to be born and its tongue was swollen and turning black. Granma lay quietly on her side, not even laboring anymore.

"We could do a Caesarian," Ancel suggested.

"On a sheep?"

"Uh-huh. You shoot her."

To kill a sheep, you draw an imaginary **X** between her eyes and ears. I said good-bye to Granma, then shot. Shot again to be sure.

Then we had to move fast, slice into her, cut the uterus, get the lamb out before the blood supply failed, and we pulled the lamb out of its mother and gripped it by the heels and swung it through the air, compressing its lungs, and it breathed, it breathed, and trembling, we laid it down beside its mother. It shook its head. Shook again. Bleated.

I picked up the gun to take it back into the house.

When her lamb bleated again, the old old ewe lifted her head, looked at her very last baby, nickered softly, and died.

The

General's

Suit

I have no taste. The very last suit I picked out for myself was rust-colored and had broad, overconfident lapels. My wife put on one of *those* faces. "I didn't know they made suits with dominoes as a lining motif," she remarked.

I do have friends more urbane than myself. Their apparel never rouses the snickers and rude jibes that invariably attend my own selections. In recent years, whenever I've needed a new suit or jacket, I've corralled a distinguished friend to help me out. In theory, I'd get more handsome clothing and they'd enjoy the pleasures of my shameless flattery. It hasn't always worked out that way.

Suit salesman: Do you like the blue, sir?

Me: I don't know. Ask my friend.

Salesman: Perhaps the herringbone?

Distinguished friend: Oh, God! Try the pinstripe again. *Anybody* can wear a pinstripe.

(Salesman sneaks a glance at his watch, sighs.)

I am built funny. Picture Mark Twain's head on Ichabod Crane's body. Now hold your mental picture to the light and crumple it. That's the idea. I can't tell you how stupid I feel on a fitting stand as two otherwise rational men jerk sleeves and pummel padding, trying to stretch precisely cut cloth over my obdurate bumps, wrists, bones.

My hobby is sheep dogs and sheep-dog trialing. Fortunately, well-dressed hombres at sheep-dog trials wear vaguely Western clothing of indifferent fit, Texas hats (the bigger, the better), and belt buckles the size of steak platters. It's a democratic sport. Ranchers with miles of acres hobnob with itinerant sheep shearers; lawyers exchange dog tips with men whose wives fill in the hard parts of their checks before they scratch their name.

Mrs. Bryan Conrad is the grande dame of American sheep-dog trialing. President of the U.S. Border Collie Club, she sponsors trials, runs her own dogs quite successfully, and has done demonstrations on the David Letterman show and before the Secretary of Agriculture. Her late husband, Brigadier General Bryan Conrad, was assigned as tactical officer to West Point three times and served as Eisenhower's Intelligence Chief during the Normandy landings. He was a splendid horseman. In 1939, he was playing polo, Mrs. Conrad remembers, when the phone call came from the war office in London. General Conrad was the first American officer attached to the British Army, and after the war, the Brits gave him an OBE for his services.

Mrs. Conrad has a low opinion of my attire, and one evening she asked if I wanted to have one of the late general's suits. Naturally, I said no.

She said, "Bryan had wonderful taste. All his suits were custom made in London."

"Yes, please," I said.

The suit's a three-piece tan job. The tweed is heavy enough

to turn small-caliber bullets. Although it's softly cut, it is rather intimidating. Just the thing to send along to an IRS audit if you don't wish to go yourself.

I feel like an imposter wearing it.

This spring I planned to fly to Britain to buy a sheep dog bitch and my wife suggested, "Why not take the suit to the tailors who made it and have it altered to fit you?"

Patiently, I explained the facts of life. "It was made in 1964, honey. Probably they're not still in business."

"Call Directory Assistance."

Two weeks later I was walking down Saville Row. London's West End is low buildings, three and four story, a village on a Dickensonian scale. Bespoke shirtmakers share premises with bespoke tailors. Creamy cards in Edwardian windows announce (discretely) "REGULAR VISITS TO THE USA." N. Huntsman and Son, Grieves and Hawkes, Anderson and Sheppard. It was drizzling, but I stayed dry under my fine white Texas hat.

Davies and Son was around the corner on Old Burlington Street. The window lights in their dark front door sparkled; somebody had polished the brass latch that morning. "May I help you, sir?"

That's Mr. Webster talking. Mr. Webster is a cordial sort of man.

The reception room was lined with bolts of fabric. Shirts were stacked in a dark cabinet, a half-dozen ties (some in regimental patterns) reposed in the showcase. Guides to the peerage perched on a shelf above the electric fire. The long socks were muted shades, un-American patterns. A few pairs of shorts peeped out beneath the shirts (boxer shorts, of course).

"Mr. Cooper will be your cutter, sir."

Mr. Cooper had straight pins in the lapel of his unassuming blue suit. The leather thong that crossed his waistcoat dipped out of sight into his pocket. I was beginning to think I'd wandered onto a set from "Masterpiece Theater." In the fitting room, I was anxiously clutching my droopy tweed pants to me when Mr. Cooper provided house braces: electric blue, thumb-wide, the sort of punk braces Sid Vicious might have admired. I blinked.

I explained the suit had been given to me, had been made by Davies and Son twenty-five years ago—could they make it fit?

Mr. Cooper winced. "We *will* make them too well, sir, won't we?"

Mr. Cooper was very quick with his chalk marks, his decisions. When I donned the waistcoat, he noted, "Usually, sir, we don't button the bottom button."

Hastily, I rectified my blunder.

The fit wasn't too far off. "We've had to do more with suits we made for our own customers," Mr. Cooper said, patting his own nonexistent paunch for explanation. Though Mr. Cooper agreed with each of my suggestions, somehow we ended up doing exactly as he wished as I basked in the glow of my own sartorial sagacity.

Before I was finished enjoying it, the fitting was done. Alterations would take three weeks. An original suit, Mr. Webster noted, would certainly require two fittings and sometimes, after a man wore it for a week or so, a third, "tuning it, so to speak," but this alteration could be accomplished with one. Mr. Webster invited me to sign their book, which I did, last in a list of distinguished names attached to posh addresses.

At the door, Mr. Webster said, "Sir, that's a lovely hat. Lovely."

I found my sheep dog, a two-year-old named Gael, in Scotland. We'd traveled together for weeks, and this morning, my last in Britain, she accompanied me. It was pouring rain in London town and Gael was sopping when I led her into the august premises of Davies and Son, Court Tailors.

When I tied her to the brass fireplace grate, Mr. Webster gave her a pat. "Well, hullo there, Lass. What's your name?"

A cutter went over to greet her, explaining, "I have a Spaniel myself, sir."

Once again, Mr. Cooper led me into the fittings room and once more produced Sid Vicious's braces.

"Thanks, I brought my own."

He smiled.

The suit fit. If you have the type of body for whom ready-mades are made, you cannot possibly understand how it feels to stand for the first time in a suit where there is cloth where it should be and no wrinkles. For the first time in my life, I looked even. The figure facing me in the full-length mirror was somebody I would have taken a check from.

"Quite nice," Mr. Cooper said.

In the quiet reception room, Gael snoozed under the showcase while I waited for the rain to stop. Davies and Son had opened their doors in 1803. They've made suits for kings, princes, dukes, lordships, and Americans like Bing Crosby, Joe Kennedy, Harry S Truman, and Brigadier General Bryan Conrad.

Mr. Webster said, "Oh no, sir, we don't advertise. It's all word of mouth. You can have too many customers, if you know what I mean, sir. When the dollar was strong against the pound, oh, we had so many international orders. We had to cut back on some of our overseas trips. We couldn't neglect our home customers, now could we, sir?

"The Davies coat will have a natural shoulder line, a bit of suppression at the waist, a soft-looking coat—not so soft as the Anderson coat, of course. I don't believe you should notice a man is well dressed until you've been talking to him for fifteen minutes. Clothes don't make the man, now do they, sir?"

When I asked about fabrics, Mr. Webster pinched my lapel. "That's twenty-three-ounce tweed, sir. You'd not find many fabrics that heavy these days. Most Americans won't have anything heavier than eight ounce. We British like ours heavier. It's true, sir, the heavier fabric doesn't wrinkle and"—he eyed my suit a trifle sadly—"they *do* wear."

Davies and Son makes suits for lawyers, financial men. "Oh no, sir. Davies doesn't get many actors. Did you see the film *Wall Street*?" Mr. Webster was visibly distressed. "They got it wrong. Far too sharp, sir. Far too sharp. Financial men don't dress like that. They wouldn't be trusted."

A fiercely mustachioed man in what I thought was a too sharp gray suit came in to book an appointment with his cutter. Every customer has his own cutter and each cutter has his own coat makers and waistcoat makers and trouser makers. "Oh no, sir. They never work for anyone but their cutter. Just isn't done. Sometimes a customer will ask to change his cutter, but that's uncommon. Two of our cutters are on the Davies board of directors. Mr. Cooper, he travels to Paris for us. I go to the United States—New York, San Francisco, Philadelphia, Baltimore, Washington, D.C." Regretfully, he notes, "None of us in the West End could get along on the home trade, sir."

In 1979, after a hundred and seventy-five years in the same premises, Davies and Son had to move. They left a rabbit warren of a building which had a special fitting room (equipped with speaking tube) for the use of King George V, and several bedrooms upstairs, installed for the convenience of nineteenth-century nobility who might have a sudden urge to lie down.

"We can only advise, sir. The customer is always right. Certain things we wouldn't do, of course. We'd suggest the customer would be better served by someone else. Suppose a customer would want a slit in the back, perhaps he'd have, well, a *protuberant* rear end, we might suggest side slits instead. . . ."

He brings down a bolt of gray flannel fabric, soft to the hand. "This is an exclusive Davies fabric, sir, but I'm afraid it'll be the last. Sixty yards is the least the mills will make up and we don't use it quickly enough."

I too feel regret. I am sorry higher rents forced them out of premises they'd occupied for a hundred and seventy-five years. Perhaps Gael would have liked a snooze in one of those bedrooms. It's odd to feel the loss of a tradition I never shared. The rain slackens into a London drizzle. Gael stretchs and yawns.

Mr. Webster asks me if he might inform me when next he comes to the States. I say he might. I am transformed into a man with a bespoke tailor, a man of taste. I ask for my bill.

Which causes surprising consternation. Mr. Webster's face falls. Of course, the bill isn't ready. He hurries into the back and confers, but they haven't even started on it. "Will it be all right if we bill you, sir?"

The thought passes through my mind: "The last man a gentleman pays is his tailor." I say, "How about a credit card?"

Which doesn't improve matters much. As he searches for the imprinter, Mr. Webster explains that credit cards are rather a new innovation at Davies and Son. He finally locates it under an old *Burke's Peerage*.

I sign the blank imprint. "I'll just put your bill on it when it's ready, if that'll be all right, sir. You can trust me."

I thought I probably could.

Jesse

When Jesse was a pup, I warned the fella who wanted her about Border Collies. Working sheep dogs are very active. They're a little too smart. If you're not going to work Jesse on livestock, you'd better find some other work for her. If you don't, she'll decide what her work is and, chances are, you won't like it.

"Uh-huh," he said.

So, three years later, Jesse's chained up day and night because every time she's off her chain, she races out to the cows and runs around them in crazy circles, barking, and he can't catch her.

I say: "But I told you."

He says: "I thought you put that stuff in them. I didn't know it was in them whether you wanted it or not." He says he's going to have Jesse put down.

It is our fault. We let another man's ignorance about sheep dogs overpower what we knew about them. It's our job if anyone has to put Jesse down.

So Anne and I took Jesse back. Anne put up big hand-printed signs on the front and back door:

DON'T OPEN DOOR!

WILD DOG INSIDE!

KNOCK AND WAIT!

The first thing Jesse did when she came in our house was jump up on the table and help herself to a snack. Oh, dear. Since she'd been chained up so long, her leg muscles were soft as apple jelly. Of course she wasn't housebroken. Back and forth she paced. Back and forth. I don't think she lay down for two days.

Jesse has honest eyes. And she so wants to do right. But honest eyes aren't enough to keep a dog alive. Most people want a low-maintenance dog—a dog they can switch on and off, a dog that doesn't make trouble. If we brought Jesse to the animal shelter, she wouldn't stand a chance.

So I decided to empower Jesse. The one thing she has going for her is the instincts that got her into trouble in the first place. Jesse can be a working stock dog, valuable to a farmer, fetching his sheep, driving them, sorting off sick sheep that need treatment. A working dog may not live the life of Riley, but who says that's what they want? Besides, a good working dog is far too valuable to be put down.

I took Jesse out to the sheep and she ran around them like a lunatic. Every time Jesse went right, I commanded her, "Go right!" When she went left, I said, "Go left!" When she finally tired and lay down, "Down!" I said. Eventually we reversed the order.

Now, after a month, Jesse drops on command, flanks left and

right, and has a rather nice fetch. She's well behaved in the house and Anne has taken down the hand-lettered warning signs.

All Jesse wants is decent work, food and water, and a quiet place to rest when it gets dark. Maybe a pat now and again. Yesterday she came over for the first time and licked my hand.

"You're welcome," I said.

Awakening the Instinct

Working livestock well—that is to say, calmly and with reasonable efficiency—takes a good dog and a person who knows stock and understands what he and the dog can do to create order. None of this comes naturally, and that's why, last Saturday, I drove down to Leo Tammi's farm with my three-year-old bitch, Silk, her seven-month-old pup, Spot, and his master, our young neighbor Mark Herwald.

Autumn is damped down in the Shenandoah Valley. The oranges and reds fade into the background. The alfalfa is still green but isn't growing much, and the orchard grass is yellowed and gone by. At daybreak, it's nice to have a sweater under your jacket, but you'll be stripped down to your T-shirt by noon.

Leo Tammi's two hundred acres aren't ten minutes from I-81, perhaps twenty minutes from Harrisonburg, Virginia, and many of the farms have already been subdivided. The ground is scarred with new excavations, and two-story Colonial ranch houses perch on every hilltop. The older farmhouses are generally located somewhat lower, where the spring water is and where they avoid the worst weather.

Between the ten-acre tracts, where every man's a king, are strips of woodland and overgrown, brushy fields held for future development. It's wilder than it was when fewer people lived here.

Leo is one of those farmers the Soil Conservation boys choose to put on their demonstrations of no-till planting and "turnips for late-season forage." Judy, his wife, has the mail route and generally takes their two-year-old son, Aaron, with her on her rounds.

Their lane dips down at the mailbox, through acres of alfalfa and closely grazed sheep pasture. Leo uses electric fence to divide his pastures even though that makes for problems with his dogs. Border Collies are goosey at best, and once they get a jolt, there's no telling what they'll do.

Neither Mark, my young companion, nor Spot had ever worked stock before and this was their first stock-dog clinic. At home, Spot was fascinated by sheep. He hunkered down and glared at them in the hunting attitude shepherds have transmuted over the years into a more useful attitude: herding. Spot is big for a Border Collie, perhaps fifty pounds. He's rangy and handsome. Looking at him, it's hard to remember he's just a puppy.

Sheep-dog clinics and trials are social occasions, too, and I know many of the people here and more of the dogs. Jack Knox, the instructor, was born in Scotland and came to the States fifteen years ago. Some students raise cows, some hogs, several raise sheep. One fellow raises range turkeys and uses his dog to load the birds on their fateful day. The clinic begins at nine, breaks for a potluck lunch, and resumes until all the dogs have run twice, generally about five o'clock.

There are more dogs than people—Hope, Molly, Tess, Bill, Judy, Mirk, Florence, Belle, and Socks. These are the dogs I know.

Both Silk and Spot were up in the seat when we pulled in. Silk enjoys these events enormously. Spot just hoped to get out of the car, where he'd thrown up twice. His eyes were worried, vague.

The dogs tied to the training ring were big, little, prick-eared, flop-eared, long- and short-coated, black and white, brown. Spot had never seen so many dogs *like* him, and his tail curled over his back as he tugged at Mark's lead, sniffing, making acquaintances. Since Silk was in heat, I left her in the car.

The ring where the young dogs start is snow fence, perhaps fifty feet across. At one end, it's attached to Leo's barn, where the sheep await their turn. The sheep are white-faced ram lambs, each about a hundred pounds. When they get excited, young dogs will often nip the sheep, and throughout the two-day clinic, Leo makes good-natured jokes—"Watch the testicles." But he holds an eighty-dollar sheep-damage check from every student handler, just in case.

In the ring are four sheep, student handler and dog, and Jack Knox and his dog Hope, who he uses to keep the sheep off the fence. That ring is crowded at times. Spectators line the fence. Some take notes. Some have cameras. Jack Knox is a sturdy, light-haired man, not yet forty. Though his Scottish burr is slight, at first Mark had a little trouble understanding him.

Working dogs must know at least six commands: "Go left," "Go right," "Stop," "Walk up on your sheep," "Come to me," and "Get back." "Get back" is the most important single command because that cry transmutes hunting into herding. The dog circles the sheep, threatening them with his mesmerizing eye, but when the dog dives in for the kill, the handler cries, "Get back!" and the dog resumes circling. The distance thus imposed, Jack Knox says, "Give your dog room to listen and think."

The handler stands in the ring shooing the sheep while the dog circles, first one way, then the reverse. Each time the dog darts in for a bite, the handler cries it off. It sounds simpler than it is.

Border Collies are slow-maturing dogs, and until they reach

puberty, they don't have the single-minded fascination with sheep that allows you to train them. It's wonderful to be there the day a young dog first "sees" sheep. His ruff goes up, his tail drops, he hunkers down—in that instant, he finds his life's work. Until the dog "sees" sheep, his instincts are dormant; sheep might as well be woolly, animate pieces of furniture.

Spot is much taller than his mama or poppa, and maybe he's put all his energy into growing because, despite his size, he's puppyish. When Mark takes off his lead in the ring, Spot passes right by the sheep to introduce himself to Hope. Hope, who is working livestock, won't give Spot the time of day, so he runs to the edge of the ring and introduces himself to the dogs tied to the palings.

When Jack Knox stirs the sheep, Spot doesn't care. He shuns them and continues his social rounds. Jack puts him back on the lead and brings him in closer, and Spot fights the lead. "Don't just walk along, dragging him," Jack says. "Let the lead go slack, and then jerk it. If he keeps on fighting, jerk it again." Jack makes noises to excite sheep and dog, whistles, calls, claps hands, creating excitement he hopes will be infectious.

Spot wants no part of it. He follows the stranger holding his lead but tangles himself in Jack's legs, wearing his most endearing puppy smile. After ten minutes of this, Jack ties him to the fence, hoping the speeding sheep and general hurly-burly might awaken his instincts.

It's a tough morning, but that doesn't spoil Mark's appetite. At noon, everybody lines up for baked ham, homemade bread, rice and pea casserole, potato salad, apple sauce, and plenty of desserts. Fastened in the shade beside the car, Spot ate his Purina Dog Chow.

Spot clearly viewed the training ring as an unfortunate, non-repeatable aberration in his puppy life. Spot was magnanimous, ready to forgive Mark for putting him in there. Certainly, he didn't expect to go back. That afternoon, as soon as Mark removed his lead, Spot tried to jump the snow fence. Jack caught him in time and dragged him back.

Each year, Jack Knox gives dozens of stock-dog clinics in the United States and Canada. Last weekend, Jack was in Montana; next weekend, he'll be in Missouri. Usually, his wife accompanies him, and their pickup truck tows a neat silver trailer containing nineteen of their own dogs. Jack spoke about an Aussie trainer he's seen: "First thing this fellow does is hold the dog down, just kneels on it until it quits wriggling. Or he lifts the dog up, holds it an inch from his face and yells. He wants to achieve dominance. I don't believe in that. I want respect from a dog. Ask your dog and give to it when it answers you." Once more he released Spot. "Spot, come here. Come here, son. That's a good boy. *Spot!!*" as Spot bolted for the fence.

That evening, when we came home, my wife asked Mark how it had gone. Mark said, "He was the worst dog there. He kept trying to jump out all the time."

On the way in the next morning, I said that maybe Spot would start to work today; I'd detected certain encouraging signs and perhaps things would go better. Spot rode on Mark's lap, underneath the shoulder harness, with his head on the console. He didn't throw up, but he drooled. In the backseat, Silk snoozed.

Right away, Spot was tied to the inside of the ring, where dogs and sheep swirled by. Most dogs were improved today and Jack felt obliged to offer a caution. "I don't want any of you people to go home and push these dogs. I'm pushing these dogs as hard as I can and I know when to stop. Trouble is, when your dog gives you an inch, right away, you people want a mile. Take the inch and be grateful for it."

Spot lay alone in the ring as the sheep thundered by along with strange dogs and strange cries. When his turn came, Jack told Mark to take off the lead. "He'll never trust you if you don't trust him."

And Spot sailed clean over that snow fence and bolted

through the Tammis's yard. He went around back of the house, where Leo had a hundred breeding ewes, and went right through them; you could chart his progress by the wake of the ewes' panic.

Spot scrambled over the woven wire into the alfalfa field, then raced along the line fence, under the ridge and the brow of the thick woods. Mark clambered after and Judy Tammi followed. A fellow in a red shirt joined the chase. (You have no idea how much faster a dog is than you are.)

The line fence was high and it looked like Spot wasn't going to be able to get into the woods. The handlers had abandoned the ring to see better, and as I drove by, I asked, "Where is he?" Jack said it looked like he was coming down toward the lane. Silk and I raced up the lane, hoping to intercept the puppy or, failing that, head him off.

Half a mile along, we stopped. I couldn't see anything, but I heard a dog barking. There were houses behind the woods and maybe Spot had stirred up another dog.

At home, it wouldn't be so dangerous. Once the terrified pup recovered his wits, he could find his way back. At home, everybody knows the Herwalds and their dog.

Here it was bad. For Spot, this was all alien ground. Every scent, every aspect, was totally unfamiliar, and if he got far enough out, there was a good chance Mark would never see him again.

Silk and I bustled through the fields. Leo has many small fields and has fenced all of them. Later on, I complimented Leo on the number of his fences. Silk jumped through or over most of them. I dropped her over the tall ones.

I heard Judy Tammi call, "He's running the horses!"

Horses? Wonderful.

Silk preceded me into a fine ridge-top pasture, and an instant later I saw Spot. He was bounding along at a good clip. A horse wheeled over the horizon and dipped back. Another horse came over the top, headed for Silk. "That'll do, Silk! Silk, no!"

Silk pursues livestock. She does not understand when livestock pursue her, and wants to turn and make a fight of it. The first time a stock dog meets strange, big livestock, it can get rough, and I didn't want her savaging the neighbors' horses. "Silk, that'll do!"

Mark tells his story: "I heard Spot barking, but I was in the woods and couldn't see anybody. And then this big horned animal, like a big goat, got up and ran away." (A buck deer hiding out from bow hunters?) "And then I came out into this field and I saw Spot and I saw Silk, and this horse started chasing Silk and me, so I ran and I jumped right over this fence into this lady's flower garden—I think it was her horses—and she came out and said, in this *real* snotty voice, 'Can I help you?' and I said I was just trying to catch my dog and jumped back over the fence."

Spot had had his fill of adventure for one day. When he saw me and Silk, standing quietly, he came right over and allowed me to fasten a lead to his collar.

The horses were less anxious to quit. They were young horses, and after having this dog amongst them, chasing and barking, their blood was up. They ran at me and the dogs, and when I flipped my cap in their faces, one got up on his hind legs and lashed out with his hooves. Judy Tammi fended off the horses while Mark and I got the dogs.

We crashed downhill through the woods, sliding on the matted leaves, and I didn't turn Silk loose until we were over the fence in the field. My car wasn't far. I drove. Mark rode in back with the dogs.

The handlers were standing beside the lane, waiting, and as we came up, I held two fingers out the window, in a **V**, and smiles wreathed their faces. They all knew how bad they'd feel if it was their young dog, in strange country, gone.

PART IV

Neighbors

Making
Enemies

Folks born in Highland County expect to die in Highland County. That's why there's not much crime. If you were a wild teenage boy, thinking to steal another man's automobile, would you do it if you'd be called "car thief" all your days? Would you burgle a country store if your act would shame your family for, say, fifty years? Country people aren't morally better than city people, they've just got to live with everything they've ever done.

Old Buck Johnson rents the farm next door. There is something pleasurable about an eighty-year-old man who brings a folding table when he comes out to visit his cows so he and his wife can have a real sit-down picnic, complete with checked tablecloth, under the apple trees.

But Buck hates to fix a fence and won't retrieve a stray cow, not even the beast who's burst through his rotten wire and is standing, foursquare, in my wife's spinach patch with a clump of greens droobling out of its mouth.

"Hello, Mr. Johnson? This is Mr. McCaig, out in Highland County. One of your cows has broke out and—"

"WHAT'S THAT YOU SAY?"

"One of your COWS is in OUR—"

"SPEAK UP, CAN'T YOU?"

"YOUR COW—"

"I DON'T HEAR SO GOOD. I'LL LET YOU TALK TO MY WIFE."

"Hello, Mrs. Johnson. Your cows are out again and there's a heifer in our vegetable garden and—"

"I'm sorry, but you'll have to talk to Buck about that."

The worst man who ever rented next to us came out one September with a truckload of prime cattle—they had number tags on chains around their necks, just like show cattle. He did brag on those cows, bragged a bit on himself, too. In December when the snow was six inches deep, he phoned us. "Uh, do you think I ought to feed my cows?"

"Folks generally do."

Every few weeks, when it was convenient, he'd bring out twenty bales of hay and those cows were so hungry they'd eat the baler twine. It was awful. The cows'd stand at the fence and moo at us as we fed our own stock, and as they gaunted up, they got sick and went down. When we phoned the owner, he'd say, "Do you know a vet?" and the vet would come and do what he could and that man never did pay that vet's bill.

We actually hated that man. We'd go into Slim's Store and curse him and tell what he'd done and people would look at us and say, "Uh-huh" and "Oh, my," and we thought they didn't care. We finally got the law on the man.

It was three years later, long after he'd gone, talk turned to him in the store, people saying what a son of a bitch he was.

If you're going to be living in a place all your life, you don't make enemies you don't need to. And when you run across someone who you know, deep down, you're not going to like, you might take three or four years just to *start* disliking them. No hurry. They're going to be an SOB all your life.

Smoke

Eaters

When I got to the firehouse, my heart sank. The rule was, the first man to arrive rolled the apparatus. Although my farm isn't a mile from the firehouse of the Bath-Highland Volunteer Fire Department, I'd never quite got there quick enough to be the man behind the wheel, first to the fire scene, in charge. Today I had been out-dawdled—and today it was a house fire.

As I rolled up the doors and started our brush truck, another car pulled up—Nevin Davis, a fine man, but no spring chicken. Nevin was no more eager to be in charge than I was.

Ninety percent of the fires we fought were grass or wood lot fires. We had a few chimney fires; occasionally a barn or outbuilding. House fires were quite rare and, of course, house fires were what mattered. When a homeowner bought a book of our raffle tickets or made a donation, when firemen came out on their own time to train or practice on the apparatus, nobody was worried about grass fires. Home fires are a volunteer fire department's reason for being—and its greatest fear.

Like a coward, I asked Nevin, "You know how to drive this thing?" Nevin peered down the road, hoping for someone full-witted to show up.

"Nope," he said. The bees droned over the Queen Anne's lace by the roadside.

"Okay," I said.

In those days, the Bath-Highland VFD's brush truck was a 1943 Burma Jeep with an open cab; the driver perched up front beside the motor. The fire-fighting equipment—a three-hundred-gallon tank, ladders, hose reels, and (vitally important) air packs—rode in the back. The Burma Jeep had four forward speeds and two axles. The shift pattern and special instructions were up on the transmission housing, right where any fool could see it. "You tell me where to shift," I told Nevin.

The first gear I caught was too high for a smooth start, but once we came careening down the Williamsville Hill, we picked up speed. Driving a fire truck loaded with water is a unique experience: You rock and slosh on all the corners.

"Up and to the right," Nevin directed me as I shifted.

"What next?" I shouted. It's windy in a cabless fire truck, and loud, and I was sick with worry. Whenever a citizen phoned in a fire call to the Bath-Highland VFD, ten telephones ran simultaneously. Some phones, like the one in Slim's Store, generally had a few fellows hanging about them; others jangled in farmhouses that were empty, since all the family was out in the barn or putting up hay. So you never knew who'd answer, only that someone would, and that someone would race the truck to your home. This time that someone was me.

The fire was at a two-story frame house, a big tinderbox, and I knew there were two children at home: a baby and an infant still in his playpen. With the air packs we were carrying, a man could walk right into a fire—which was what I was thinking about, on account of those children.

Like other volunteers, I'd been on professional training exercises inside burning buildings. They are frightening and appalling. It's literally hellish in there. Except for the hottest flames (faint flickers in the blackness), you can't see a thing. You crawl along the hose line, toward the heat and steam, afraid to get lost.

"Gear down!" Nevin advised as we lugged up the fish hatchery hill.

I was trying to remember what I'd learned about the air pack. It'd been six months since last I had it on. Should I check the flow lever or was it set for constant demand? How did you clear your face mask?

The children's bedroom was on the second floor, and the quickest way to it would be up the front stairs or over the porch roof if the interior stairs were enveloped. Was their bedroom the first or second on the left?

In a fire, frightened children often hide. They'll crawl into a closet or underneath the bed or behind the furniture. Proper procedure is to enter the room and grope around the perimeter, feeling behind and on top and beneath furniture for anyone unconscious lying there.

"Watch it!" Nevin said as we wailed past a tractor and haywagon that couldn't move over quick enough.

I was watching ahead for the pillar of smoke in the clear sky to tell us how bad it was.

I geared down (what a nasty clatter!) to make the turn at the bottom of their lane. The lane clung to the side of a hill, and if the brush truck ever slipped out of the ruts, it wouldn't stop tumbling until . . . I floored the gas, bounced over the hilltop, slalomed by the farm equipment. A wide white wooden gate hung half open at the entrance to the yard. Like Smokey and the Bandit, I bored right through, rode that gate down under my bumpers, and thundered into their front yard, siren shrieking.

The husband stood on the lawn, his wife beside him. One child held her hand, the infant was safe in her arms. When my siren died, it left a hole big enough to hide in.

Behind us, way down the road, a second siren was coming.

"The fire's out," the father said.

Many fire insurers won't insure my house. We heat with wood, the stone chimneys are unlined, what wiring I haven't replaced is quite old, and because we don't have a continuous foundation (the house is up on posts), a grass fire can get underneath the whole shebang.

Inevitably, during the spring, we'll make some hay that's too green. We stack the bales individually on the barn floor and check them daily for heating. Spontaneous-combusting green hay has leveled many a fine wooden barn.

Our five-hundred-gallon tank of gasoline is behind our workshop. Inside the shop are grease and oil, paint, turpentine and thinners, ether (to start the tractor on cold mornings), and other volatile fluids.

Thus, like many another country dweller, I am a fire paranoid. I figure our house is still standing after a hundred twenty years because previous owners were fire paranoids, too.

Seventeen years ago, when we moved onto the farm, the nearest volunteer fire department was an hour away and not much use except for wetting down the ashes. So when some neighbors started talking about a fire department, Anne and I were enthusiastic. Robert Lockridge donated land for a firehouse. Green Valley Farm lent us their backhoe. Augusta Block, in Staunton, gave us a good price on concrete blocks (if we picked them up), and whenever a farmer took cows into market, he'd swing by the block yard to load up. There were always a few loafers at Slim's store who'd help unload them.

Joe Meszaros, who has a weekend camp here, donated the

overhead doors, and some Burnville roofers put on the standing-seam metal roof.

The Peaceful Valley Hunt Club located a pair of ancient fire trucks (our other truck was a 1953 Dodge pumper) and some cast-off fire-fighting gear. We bought two air packs spanking new: eight hundred dollars each.

The eight thousand dollars everything cost us was raised by donations, dances, a watermelon feast, a dreadful number of chicken barbecues, and an outright grant from the Bath County Supervisors.

We'd started talking about it in the spring. By winter, the roof was on our two-bay firehouse, and we had two trucks filled with water and gasoline and ready to go. The Bath-Highland Volunteer Fire Department (rather to everyone's surprise) had become a reality.

The western part of Virginia, bordering Bath and Highland counties, is mountainous, and the big landowners here are the George Washington National Forest and the Virginia Game Commission. Except during hunting season, folks are few and far between. Williamsville (pop. 12) has the store and the church and the post office. The post office serves eighty-six mailboxes in an area of a hundred and fifty square miles. Bath-Highland has one of the smallest fire departments in the state, but it is typical of the fire departments that provide protection in rural areas all over the country.

Like much of rural America, what had been an integrated mix of farms and small communities is declining. Most new property owners are buying for recreation. There's nothing wrong with recreational people except they're not usually here and they've replaced people who were. As the year-round population declines, community institutions fold.

The Bath-Highland Volunteer Fire Department was the first new institution in many years. Besides the Williamsville Presbyterian Church, it is the *only* community institution. Our schools, banks, and agricultural suppliers are all in the county seat, one bad mountain and forty-five minutes away. If the VFD didn't put on dances, there wouldn't be any. The same goes for the community suppers.

All that said, there are difficulties, too. The fire company is too small. Sam Burke, the present chief, hopes to keep fifteen active members so he can field five fire fighters day or night. Mountain people are disputatious, and family feuds and cultural clashes sometimes surface in fire department meetings. The chief and president do more than their share of the work, and burnout is common.

Fighting fires is complex and sometimes hazardous. Mobile-home fires are particularly bad on account of the fumes from plastics, and mobile homes are the most common affordable housing in the countryside.

Bath-Highland's district borders the Hot Springs VFD on the north, the Millboro VFD on the southeast, and the McDowell VFD on the east. Usually, big fires are fought jointly.

At the October meeting, held in the Williamsville Community Center, a handful of people gathered to direct the department's activities. The principal business was choosing a nominating committee for upcoming elections.

Because the nominating committee would seize this opportunity to not be nominated themselves, it was important that real candidates for officer positions be kept off that committee.

The women's auxiliary said they'd bought a certificate of deposit in the amount of $1,620.06, which they'd use for the kitchen of the new firehouse if and when the men ever got around to building it.

A veteran's organization had offered the department a free American flag, which everybody was inclined to accept until someone pointed out that either (a) someone would have to raise and lower the flag each day or (b) they'd have to light it at night. "Some folks want to give you a horse, too," one member noted.

There'd been vandalism at the firehouse, two bullets fired through the doors, but luckily they hadn't hit anything. Spent cartridges were turned over to the Bath County Sheriff. "I know who that fellow is," somebody said. "One day we'll catch him at it."

A contribution can had been passed for David DuJordan, the victim of a recent fire. The department would turn over sixty-two dollars and twenty cents.

I asked Sam Burke how effective the department was. "If we can get there in ten or fifteen minutes, we can do some good," he said. "It isn't the distance, it's the mountains that slow us down." To better the odds, over the years the department has sold smoke detectors and fire extinguishers to the community at cost. In winter months, when elderly souls can't clean their chimneys, department members often do it for them.

Sam is a full-time farmer on a twelve-hundred-acre hay and cattle spread. Before he moved here, he was with the Virginia Beach VFD for twelve years. Sam's a professional. He fought to upgrade the old equipment and believes that Bath-Highland's present apparatus is second to none. (We have given the Burma Jeep to a start-up department in the north of the county.) Sam's managed to get paging devices for the active members, more and better air packs, a portable generator, and even a leaf-blower, which cleared a fire trail so fast, "those Millboro fellas just stood by watching."

Still, the key element in any volunteer fire department isn't the equipment, it's the volunteers. Sometimes I think the most important function new equipment serves is to keep the volunteer interest high.

If you've ever stood by a fire raging out of control, praying to hear that siren come down the road, you've developed a real appreciation for men and women willing to drop everything and come to the aid of a neighbor. Or as the first chief, Randolph Hodge, put it, "If you're going to be a fire fighter, you got to answer the calls. Don't matter what you think of the man whose property's burning, don't matter if you and him haven't spoken in years, you still got to fight his fire."

The George Washington National Forest runs through the southern end of both Bath and Highland counties, so the Bath-Highland VFD signs a contract every year with the Forest Service to provide men and pumpers for fires. In Virginia, volunteer fire departments are the Forest Service's first line of defense.

My wife's birthday is in June, and one year we'd arranged a double birthday party with a friend. We'd marinated shish kebabs and he brought Greek salad, and a keg of beer was cooling beside the back door. I was wearing my brightest Hawaiian shirt.

We'd just put the shish kebabs on skewers when the fire alarm rang. There were a half-dozen other firemen at the party. We looked at one another. We griped. We went.

Our ancient trucks lumbered up Shenandoah Mountain toward the thick pillar of greasy smoke. The grades were steep and the drivers kept one worried eye on the temperature gauges.

A company of cadets from a nearby military academy had been playing war games in the bone-dry forest. The ambush platoon had attacked the scout platoon and fired flares (yes, flares) to mark their position.

When we belched to a stop most of the way up the mountain, fifty or sixty teenaged soldiers were scurrying around. The fire was spread across eight or ten acres by then and was racing straight uphill, so we went up fast in two four-man teams, clearing a firebreak: The first man cuts the big stuff, the second the lesser stuff, the third sweeps the leaves with his fire rake, and the fourth gets whatever the first three have missed. Our teams pressed on uphill through acrid clouds of smoke. We didn't put on fire gear. It was hot enough already.

As we came over the ridge top and turned the fire, the Forest Service called in its aerial fire fighter, a converted DC-3, which came in low over the ridge spewing fire-suppressant chemical out of its tanks.

One volunteer eyed the plane and said, "I don't eat chemicals, I sure as hell ain't going to breathe them." As the cadets cheered the approaching bombing run, about half of the Bath-Highland VFD bolted upwind.

If you imagine we were annoyed at the cadets, you'd be right. Our hands and faces were black, teeth gritty, and our party clothes didn't look festive anymore. Because they'd touched off the blaze, the cadets would stay out in the woods tonight to guard the fire and keep it from jumping our fireline. The cadets had been out in the woods three nights already, and had been scheduled to go home. Did the prospect of their misery fill us with compassion? No, not much.

As we walked down the mountain, we talked, rather loudly, about the party we were going back to: Greek salad, um, um; how fine a cold beer would taste; and so on. The cadets were strung all along the fireline looking glum. As I climbed onto the brush truck, a plaintive teenage cadet's voice called after me, "And, sir, will there be girls?"

Power

As I write this, our power's been out twenty-four hours. It's not unusual. Every month or two, some natural calamity knocks lines down in the Virginia highlands, and it sometimes takes a week before it comes back on.

It's not too bad. We've got springs where we can draw water, our cookstove uses gas, and we heat with wood. The biggest problem is the freezers, which we swaddle in space blankets and down sleeping bags so they don't thaw.

The best of no electricity is the quiet. No hum of refrigerator motors, no whoosh as the gas water heater ignites, no whine of the water pump. Our farmhouse is an old log house, and for a hundred years, people must have sat in this kitchen talking quietly with no sound louder than the songbirds outside, the crackle of the fire, maybe the solemn tick of a mantel clock. News was what your neighbor told you. Right now, our news is that the electric co-op trucks have been seen just down the road in Williamsville.

It wasn't until 1948 the REA put electricity down our valley, and first place farmers wanted it was the barn—for the electric milking machine. When power did come into the house, they'd string a line across the ceiling until it stopped and dangled, bare bulb, right above the farmer's favorite reading chair.

The electricity people promised to relieve the farm family of drudgery. With no clothes to scrub or kerosene lamps to clean or water to tote, everybody could lean back and take it easy. If you ask the old people how it was before the electricity, they'll talk about quilting bees and homecomings and how they used to come calling on a Sunday afternoon. Nobody seems to remember the drudgery.

Without electricity, it gets dark in the house very early. We read by candle or kerosene lamp; the TV sits mute in the corner. Tonight I think I'll bring out a deck of cards. Perhaps Anne and I can play cribbage, or hearts, or pinochle, or bezique.

Neighbors

I was checking my bags at the Delta counter in Roanoke when they handed me a message.

"Thank goodness you called," Anne said. "Our pump just quit."

It had been droughty since August, our stock ponds were dry, and every day we watered a hundred ten milking ewes and ninety lambs. Not to mention the water for six dogs, flushing the toilet, and washing the supper potatoes. Our farm is fifty-five minutes from the nearest supermarket, an hour from a hospital, forty-five from the nearest decent automobile wrecking yard. Electrical parts, welding rods, lamb medications: fifty-five minutes. Well driller: sixty-five minutes. Plumber: sixty.

Anne added, "Barry is here. He thinks it's the foot valve."

A shallow well foot valve attaches to the bottom of the well pipes, some eighty feet underground. To replace it, you must lift the well cover, unbolt the well seal, drag all the stiff heavy pipe out of the well, wrench the foot valve off the pipe, reverse the entire process, prime the pump, and hope it goes.

"Okay," I said, "I'll call you after I land in Seattle," and boarded my flight and thought no more about it. Barry Marshall is a good neighbor.

Farming as we do, living where we do, we couldn't make it without neighbors. The American frontier mythos, "Don't tread on me" and "I'd rather die than owe a man a favor," was always honored more in the breach than the observance. Without our neighbors we'd toss in the towel in six months.

At the end of the day, when I finally called home, Anne reported that Barry had driven into town for the valve (round trip: two hours, ten minutes), then he and Jim Stone had pulled the pipes, replaced the valve, and had the well pumping again by five. For their trouble, they charged forty dollars (plus parts).

It works both ways: When neighbors call on us for help, we drop what we're doing, too. Our '53 Dodge Power Wagon has a stout winch equipped with a half-inch steel cable and can fetch most vehicles out of the ditch. We've gotten a few hesitant knocks on our door after midnight, but most good neighbors wait until morning.

Five years ago in February, a pickup with three hunters in it skidded off the state road in the Bullpasture Gorge and a hundred fifty feet down the cliff, into the river. Since the nearest rescue squad is an hour away in good weather (it took them two hours that night), both young and old men waded into the hip-deep icy water to pull injured and dead out of that truck. Afterward, there was a lot of discussion whether we should form our own community rescue squad, but with so few citizens, we feared we wouldn't make a good job of it. Instead, we invited an instructor from the county seat to come down to our community center to teach us basic and advanced first-aid techniques. Thirty-five people sat through that course and everybody got their Red Cross certificates.

If I seem to be describing an ideal human community, I don't mean to. Though we are bonded by necessity, our community contains all the usual discontents and cherished resentments. Sometimes necessity forces a tolerance that blossoms into affection, but, of course, it can have the opposite effect. Formal country manners are the lubrication that enable people who don't really care for one another to cooperate in what needs to be done.

Like many Appalachian communities, ours is socially rigid. Not much gets done here without the backing of the old families. Other important social distinctions include property owners and non–property owners, churchgoers and non, teetotalers and drunks (the community doesn't admit the possibility of social drinking). One subgroup unique to our valley is a group I think of as "Lost Boys." They are akin but not identical to "Good Ol' Boys."

The Lost Boys grew up in the valley, moved away, had successful jobs or small businesses, and when, in midlife, things fell apart for them (starting with their marriages), they returned. Here, there're always hunting camps needing a caretaker, plenty of deer meat to eat, heaps of fish in the rivers, and no nagging woman to tell them how much Old Milwaukee to drink. Hank Williams, Jr., is their favorite singer, particularly his tune "A Country Boy Can Survive."

Despite this machismo, most of the Lost Boys are gentle souls, maudlin drunks, seeking our Power Wagon to pull them out of the ditch more often than most. Since we always need hay help in the summer months, we hire Lost Boys when we can't find teen-agers looking for work. Although the teenagers don't know as much, the Lost Boys' fondness for Old Mill makes them less reliable hay hands. And besides, I confess it discomforts me to buck hay bales with a man my age (fifty) who has been divorced (as I have), had his own small business (like mine), and lost it all. Country manners pretend these fellows aren't working for wages but out of pure neighborliness. "Oh, I suppose I could come down and help you out"—that's what they say.

Unlike Good Ol' Boys, Lost Boys retain reentry rights to the respectable world. After a year or two in the valley, most of them tire of deer meat and poverty and go back to urban life, take up a new job, remarry. Our particular breed of Good Ol' Boys are more hopeless. They're the fellows we see shamefacedly hoofing it down the road because they've been DUI'd so many times, next time they get caught it's the penitentiary. When they do sneak behind the wheel, their wheels never touch a road that's paved. Most are quite meek.

David Massey is less passive than most of the Good Ol' Boys, able (and willing) to say exactly the wrong thing at just the right time. He once grilled a Jewish neighbor about the expression "Jew him down." "I mean, Mel, just what does it mean? Who can I ask if I can't ask you, huh?" Alas, not every poet writes poetry.

When local young people quarrel with their families and march noisily out of the house, they beeline to the Lost Boys for shelter. Like Dutch uncles, the Lost Boys warn the young away from deadly hazards, jump-start their old cars, tolerate these kids' deep goofiness, their hormones gone wild. I've never known a Lost Boy to exploit one of these kids, though they surely get drunk with them from time to time. Nobody's gonna tell these kids how much Old Mill they can drink either.

I didn't know Carleton Grant was going to court until the day they convicted him, although the grapevine had been buzzing with his case for weeks. Uniformly, our community blamed Carleton's ex-wife.

For years, Carleton owned a pump and tank company in Staunton, on the other side of the mountain. He was a master electrician and plumber, and he installed gasoline tanks for gas stations and farms. If Barry Marshall hadn't come over the day our pump went out, Anne would have called Carleton next. When the EPA announced new regulations for underground gas tanks, Carleton's insurance climbed to twenty thousand dollars a year. He'd gotten injured somehow and there was some sort of insurance claim pending, but I never understood much about that part of it. Carleton and his wife separated, then divorced, and he started playing Hank Williams tapes, loud. He moved into a decrepit house in Williamsville, fixed it up some, but when the Kincaid place came vacant, a mile above us, he moved in there. It's a two-story frame house on a couple acres with indoor water and outdoor johnny house. Carleton kept two horses there, a goat and a dog. After Thanksgiving, he hung a Christmas wreath on his front door.

He did some wiring for us, plumbed and wired for some other folks. He spent most of last summer working with Jerry Burns, who farms with horses. Carleton had a real fondness for old-timey ways. He was a buckskinner for a hobby. These buck-skinners are black-powder enthusiasts who, every summer, rendezvous in remote locations to fire their rifles, hurl tomahawks, and swap replicas of the mountain men's gear they've carefully crafted over the winter. They drink a bit of Old Milwaukee, too.

Carleton looked like a mountain man—squat, with powerful chest and arms, black beard, and longish hair flecked with gray. He was a man with considerable personal authority. Once, I was talking with Barry Marshall about a couple of squabbling neighbors. Their quarrel had reached the point where stupidity was compounding stupidity and something bad was due to happen. "Don't worry," Barry grinned, "Carleton will settle it." And I thought that, on balance, he would.

I never did meet Carleton's wife. One neighbor says she is a "B–I–T–C–H," but a woman I trust said she'd met her and she seemed "right nice."

One drunken afternoon, last spring, David Massey marched right into Carleton's kitchen, where Carleton was sitting sharpening his bowie knife. Apparently David started in with his mouth. Carleton told him to leave, told him again, told him again, smacked him. Community consensus was (a) it was okay for Carleton to hit David, (b) it was good he hit him with the whetstone instead of the knife, (c) he probably should have stopped hitting him before he did. David took seventy-two stitches.

Mrs. Stephenson, up on Tower Hill, is eighty years old and remembers Carleton's daddy. She said he used to beat the boy, just whip him awful. Carleton once said he wouldn't ever be hit again, not by no man.

When the case finally came to court, David testified that he didn't recall what had happened that day, that he'd been too drunk to remember. Disgusted, the judge dismissed the charges but warned them to stay away from each other. The local kids said Carleton was okay so long as he was drinking beer, but you had to watch out when he started on the whiskey.

Me and Timmy Marshall (Barry's brother) were cutting firewood when we learned that Carleton Grant had been found guilty of sexually abusing his daughter and had been sentenced to thirty years. I was upset and Timmy, who'd known Carleton better than me, was stunned. We talked about it, every break we took, all day. In Williamsville, in the store, nobody believed it. They said it was because the jury was mostly women. They said it was because his ex-wife was out to get him. When Timmy called Carleton that evening in the Staunton jail, Carleton was confident—that his daughter would change her story, that he'd get out on appeal. Carleton's nephew and some friends started moving Carleton's stuff out of the Kincaid house into storage in Williamsville. Up and down the road they drove, up and down. Somebody took the horses away, somebody took the goat. I don't know who got Carleton's dog. A buckskinner friend collected Carleton's blackpowder rifle. "It's the only valuable thing Carleton has," he said.

Carleton's daughter had testified that he'd been abusing her since she was five years old. She broke down and cried in court. She said she used to pull her blanket over her when she heard him coming up the stairs. After Carleton's daughter testified, Carleton's lawyer wanted to seek a plea bargain: He'd do a year. Carleton said no, he hadn't done a thing.

It is easy to exaggerate the differences between our remote mountain community and the urban neighborhood where, perhaps, you live. But we are more like you than unlike. The questions we asked, our reactions, weren't so very different than Michael Milken's friends, or Oliver North's. "He couldn't really have done those things. It was misinterpreted. He was tricked, or trapped. He's been made a scapegoat. He was a man who did more good than harm."

One of Carleton's friends said the jury was hard on him because "anybody who looks like Carleton does has purely got to be guilty."

One of our neighbors is gone and we are less because of it. I won't judge him. I wouldn't know how.

I suspect that, in time, Carleton will become one of the valley legends. In the retelling, he'll become a finer shot than he was and, I fear, a worse monster. Although he'll be eligible for parole in eight years, nobody really expects him to come back. The snow lies smooth and even in the yard where his horses were fed. Just yesterday as I was driving past the Kincaid house, I found myself thinking about Carleton's daughter, lying terrified, listening to his footsteps on the stairs. The Christmas wreath is still hanging on his front door.

Testifying

I'd like to tell you how I came to testify before Congress. Congress wanted to strengthen the Animal Welfare Act, to make the life and death of laboratory animals somewhat less painful, and for some reason the Farm Bureau was against it. I was asked to represent all those farmers who think that lab animals should be decently treated and only join the Farm Bureau because they sell the cheapest truck insurance.

I got out the suit I wear to weddings and funerals. After some thought, I put on the funeral tie.

You've seen that committee room on TV: real tall ceilings, padded green leather chairs, those nifty desk lamps, congressmen at their high desk asking hot questions. What they don't show is this: When there's no TV, there're no congressmen either. They've got business elsewhere. All of us testifying that day spoke, for the record, to a long empty desk with a dozen empty microphones on it. Empty microphones look like snakes.

The committee chairman, George Brown, was there. He seemed like a nice guy.

Still, that committee room has terrific dignity. We spoke in whispers. We were citizens of a great democracy, come to petition our government.

I'd heard about lobbyists, and here they were. Expensively dressed, slick as butter, at ease in that room in a way we mere citizens never would be. They said no laboratory animal was being mistreated, no. And if animals were in pain, it was just an itty bitty pain. Anyway, all the abuses had been corrected. Or would be tomorrow.

They made me mad. They were so cool and I was hot and I felt stupid. Anyway, when my turn came, I stood up and said my piece and hoped it did some good, and maybe it did because afterward Congress did strengthen the law.

At noon, we broke for lunch, and we animal welfare types were standing in the corridor wondering where to go because the congressional cafeteria was reserved for congressmen and their staffers over the lunch hour. A guard—he was a great big fella—came up to me and said, "Say, ain't you Donald McCaig from Butte, Montana?"

"Yeah."

"You got a sister Carol. Right?"

"Yeah."

"Jeez, I'll be darned. I went to school with Carol. How's she doin'?"

I said Carol had a couple of kids now. She lives out in Seattle.

"Well, whaddaya know."

And that guard took all us animal welfare people right past the guy at the cafeteria door—"They're okay. They're with me"—and we got to eat lunch with the congressmen. It's good to have friends in high places.

Democracy

The Monday before Election Day was abnormally quiet here in Highland County. Usually, opening day of the Virginia turkey season is a ruckus of shots and halloos, but today the great black-and-tan birds roosted in the dripping hemlocks or squabbled through the autumn olive unmolested. You couldn't get to them. It had been raining all weekend, and the Simmonses' rain gauge, which Nelson Simmons emptied Sunday night at bedtime, overflowed Monday. It's a good deep rain gauge, too: twelve inches. The turkey hunters stayed in camp or prowled the roads, restless and discouraged. By noon they couldn't cross any watercourse in the county except where the state bridges cross. The Cowpasture River divided our farm. Monday morning you could hear it roar half a mile away.

It's not really something you expect. Probably a half-dozen times a year the TV broadcasts flood warnings. The worst it gets is deep puddles in Laurel Gap where the road dips beside the river, so maybe you postpone your trip to town until the next day.

Most of the people who died in this flood died of disbelief. They really couldn't believe it was happening.

I was worried about the election. It's twelve miles from our farm to the Varners' house in Headwaters, where the precinct votes. I'm Headwaters' precinct captain. In a precinct that votes sixty-eight souls, being captain isn't a real *big* job, but it does mean you have to drive up to Monterey, the county seat, the Saturday before Election Day so Maxine Huffman, the registrar, can give you cardboard boxes containing ballots, poll books, summaries of results, forms for "Disputed Voters," forms for "Absentees Who Wish to Vote in Person," the *Handbook for Election Officials,* two pencils, two blue ballpoints, and one red one.

Usually, the night before the election, I make up a lunch and fill a thermos of coffee. Country manners say we shouldn't *count* on a supper invitation from Orpha Mae Varner, but come 6:00 P.M. the three election officials are invariably seated at table with the Varner family, enjoying country-fried steak with gravy and Orpha Mae's homemade rolls. If a voter comes in during supper, we excuse ourselves from the table and go into the living room to vote him.

I generally figure on rising at five, election morning, and get to Headwaters by half-past, plenty of time to set up the ballot box and do the necessary swearing in. But this year it looked as though it would be poor traveling. Maybe I'd have to take the Power Wagon. Our 1951 Dodge Power Wagon has four-wheel drive and is high enough off the road that the running boards tap a tall man's knees. Its top speed is about 45 mph, and it gets eight miles a gallon at any speed. Nothing much stops it, but it rides more like a buckboard than a limousine. Tomorrow, in that old monster, grinding along wet roads in poor visibility, I'd want to leave a half an hour early.

The rain was steady but not hard as my stock dog Pip and I went down to the river field where our ewes were grazing. The perimeter ditches were over my rubber boots and running fast.

The river was out of its banks; it had climbed to within a foot of our line fence, running brown, loud, and ugly. Sheep hate to cross running water, and I thought I'd get them to higher ground before things got worse. Under the low, drizzly sky, the rye fields were as green as an Irish whiskey ad. I felt silly, overprudent, as Pip and I chivvied the bouncing sheep through the running ditches and out of the field. After the floodwaters dropped, I found dead fish in those fields, and all my fences were gone.

Our neighbors the Luxfords were in town, across the mountain in Harrisonburg, and they'd arranged for their children to be dropped off with us after school. At three-fifteen the schoolbus driver's wife called to say he couldn't get through. Since the Luxfords' kids were the last on the bus, he'd keep them at his house until the water went down.

The Varners' farm, where Headwaters Precinct votes, is an especially well-kept sheep-and-cattle operation of a hundred fourteen acres. Their house is a neat two-story frame with modest gingerbread at the eaves. Elmo Varner subscribes to all the farming journals, and when I'm being precinct captain, I usually browse through them in the long waits between voters.

Virginia's election laws are designed for great urban precincts, with voting machines and thousands of voters. They can be bruisingly awkward in Highland County, where the biggest precinct votes fewer than six hundred souls. Recently the man from the state election commissioner's office inspected Elmo's house and said Elmo would need to install a wheelchair ramp for the use of handicapped voters. Since Headwaters Precinct doesn't have any handicapped voters, that didn't sit too well. And even if we did, why, we'd be more than willing to go out and vote them in their cars. The state man said Elmo's hall-closet polling booth was acceptable, but we'd have to shift his couch and armchair to make room for a long table where the three election officials could sit elbow-to-elbow. That didn't sit too well, either.

Elections are serious here, and voter turnout is high. At the last presidential election we'd voted every single registered voter by early afternoon, except for two farmers who'd taken a load of calves to market, and young Corrinne Stewart. The farmers would stop by and vote on their way home. Corrinne had moved out to Colorado with her boyfriend and hadn't (somebody noted) written home in six months, but we had enjoyed speculating about what we'd do if Corrinne did drop out of the sky to cast her ballot. With all the registered voters voted, could we count up and go home?

Four o'clock, Monday, the river trickled into our lower fields. I decided to inspect the Luxfords' farm, just two miles east of us upriver.

The Power Wagon was built for rough conditions, and I confess to a modest thrill firing up my machine. The sky had lowered, got sullen, and I put my headlights on.

The river was within three feet of the struts of the iron bridge and across the road in Laurel Gap. Landscape features were altered, and I couldn't know whether what I was rolling across was road or jumble-tumble river bottom. I slipped the Power Wagon into low-range four-wheel drive, and we grumped along slower than a man walks. The water climbed over the running board and lapped around my feet. I heard it hiss as it spattered the engine block. The murky half-river-half-road continued on ahead as far as I could see. I put my macho machine in reverse and puttered back out of that water somewhat quicker than I'd come into it.

That night, before we lost our long-distance lines, I talked to my fellow precinct worker June Clevinger, who told me the Varners were at the Clevingers' tonight because the Varner house was under four feet of water. "Elmo just keeps getting up and looking out. He can see his rooftop from my kitchen window." June said the election would be in the church if the water didn't get it, too.

Before the power went out, about seven o'clock, the river was across the road in Williamsville, downstream from us. In Slim's Store, they moved most of the goods to upper shelves. Old Mrs. Marshall had to leave her house to stay with her daughter-in-law.

Election morning, the water at last receded, and by noon, I reached Headwaters, where we had to set up the polls.

Elmo Varner had plenty of neighbors helping at his house. The wall-to-wall carpet was lying in cut-up pieces on the front lawn. The TV was on the living-room couch, which Orpha Mae had reupholstered herself. Elmo's big John Deere tractor was powering an electric generator for the industrial vacuum cleaners and hoses being used to clear water, mud, and trash out of the devastated house.

Elmo looked as genial as a man can who hasn't slept in the last thirty hours. He said he knew he was lucky, but wished the water hadn't got into the TV.

Miller's store was closed. Without power for his coolers or gas pumps, Ronnie Miller was out of business. The water had barely lapped over the floorboards of his store, though, so he was lucky, too.

I set up the RESTRICTED AREA signs outside the Presbyterian church just as it says to do in the manual for election officers. June Clevinger was trying to get a fire going. The church has twin Warm Morning heating stoves connected by a single overhead U pipe. Normally, Orpha Mae fired these stoves an hour before services. Services are held here on alternate Sundays. According to the hymn board, attendance last week was three.

Carl Clevinger, June's husband, arranged the choir loft as a voting booth. We put our wooden pencils on one pew, figuring voters could write on the back of the pew in front of them.

For forty-seven of his seventy-three years, Carl Clevinger had been a miner in Buchanan County. He retired to his Highland hunt camp eleven years ago with June. Carl has black lung and takes spells. June Clevinger wears glasses with Coke-bottle lenses.

When they go out coon hunting at night, June does all the driving. She drives slow.

We had a couple voters waiting on us while I swore in June Clevinger, and we both signed the poll book in the spaces provided. We held up the ballot box to show it was empty before we padlocked it. The voters waited while we counted the ballots to make sure there weren't more or fewer than sixty-eight, which, fortunately, there weren't. There's a form you have to fill out when you've been given too many ballots.

We checked voters off in the poll book, and after each one voted, we took the ballot and dropped it into the green steel ballot box. Thus we ascertained that nobody had smuggled in a hundred dummy ballots with which to stuff our ballot box.

Usually Maxine Huffman gets down early with the absentee ballots, but she didn't come today. She might not have known we were open. Mrs. Simmons, the third precinct worker, called Ronnie Miller at one o'clock to say she'd be in as soon as state bulldozers cleared the landslide that had cut their house off. She arrived not much later.

Except for the moment each of us voted, I don't think any of us gave a thought to the election. All our talk was about the flood. Douglas Wilder, the first black man to run for lieutenant governor in Virginia since Reconstruction, was on the ballot, as was Mary Sue Terry, the first female candidate for attorney general, but our conversation was of US 250—how it had been washed out in Ramsey's Draft and how much worse flooding must be in Roanoke, downstream. We wondered when we'd get our power back.

Our neighbors the Luxfords came running in at three o'clock, and I told them where to find their children. They'd drowned their new diesel pickup the day before trying to get through, and had spent a bad night worrying. They did vote.

"How many does that make?" Mrs. Simmons asked.

June Clevinger counted the red checks in the poll books. "That's nine," she said.

As the afternoon wore on, the church warmed, and all the flies came out to bat at the windows. Motorists stopped at Ronnie Miller's for gas, but he explained he had no way of pumping it. They asked how bad was it ahead. People were looking after their kin and their worldly goods. Nobody was traveling for pleasure.

The voters trickled in. Neither of the Varners came in, though they are usually faithful. The tractor chugged, and the cleaners worked on at their house. June offered me a cheese sandwich and a cup of coffee. She had, she said, made extra.

We heard about Ivan Stone, whose neighbors had at first refused evacuation from their new home. There was a man, two women, and a child on that rooftop when they changed their minds and begged Ivan to please see if he could get through to take them off. Ivan tried to reach them on his tractor, but he was swept away. The family on the rooftop was lost soon afterward.

Last night about ten o'clock, Mrs. Dickenson called Bill Obaugh, the undertaker, and said her husband was dead, couldn't Bill come and get him? Bill got the volunteer fire department, and half a dozen men forded waters and scrambled along brushy hillsides to reach Mrs. Dickenson's house. At the approach of the drenched but mannerly undertaker and his team, Jack Dickenson sat up in bed and used vile language on them.

"They say he drinks a lot," Mrs. Simmons said.

Somebody spoke of a minister's wife and baby granddaughter who'd tried to get down through Franklin. They found the car but hadn't found them yet.

There wasn't much traffic on U.S. 250, and not many voters, either.

At dusk Carl Clevinger carried in a couple of kerosene lamps. They hadn't been used recently, and one was too smoky. So we had just the one lamp, which threw enough light to let us mark the poll book. If any more voters came tonight, we'd have to abandon our station so they could use the light in order to see their ballots.

At 7:01 by the fastest watch among us, we closed the polls, and all officials signed the poll books. By yellow lantern light we opened and counted the ballots. On November 5, 1985, Virginia elected Jerry Baliles governor; Douglas Wilder lieutenant governor, and Mary Sue Terry attorney general. I am pleased to note that Headwaters Precinct concurred with the wisdom of the greater electorate by a margin of nine to five.

An
Escaped
Convict

We don't get too much big-time crime in Highland County, not the kind you see on the evening news, so folks were kind of pleased when we had an escaped convict.

Convicts aren't unusual in Virginia—they've got convict gangs working on the roads. There's this little orange convict house on the highway department truck and one or two guards with shotguns, 'case any of them makes a run for it. If I was ever put in prison, I think I'd like to be on the road gang. It'd be quieter outdoors and you could take a breath of air.

Anyway, an escaped convict beelined straight for our mountains. He'd been in North Carolina prison for breaking and entering and stealing cars. His name was Ralph "Peanut" Minter. I don't expect he was real tall.

First thing anyone heard about this convict was when Trooper Greg Stump passed this car going the other way, and before it was out of sight, it suddenly started taking evasive action, which naturally made the trooper suspicious, so he turned around and pursued it. There were two people in the car, Mrs. Minter and Peanut. He jumped out when the trooper drew near and waded the Cowpasture River and disappeared in the woods.

There are tens of thousands of acres of wood here, all the woods an escaped convict could possibly want. We're short on people but long on woods.

All the state troopers and sheriff's deputies drove down here, up and down the county roads, peering out the window, trying to get a glimpse of Peanut. That afternoon, Billy Jackson was sitting on the porch when a short fellow came out of the woods, walked up, and asked did Billy have a cigarette.

Billy did.

Then Peanut introduced himself, said he was an escaped convict.

"In that case," Billy said, "you'll be wanting a match, too."

Peanut sat on the porch, smoked his cigarette, and went back in the woods.

For miles around, everybody was in a tizzy. Widow ladies bolted their doors. Farmers kept their eyes peeled, the country stores were abuzz. Escaped convicts, past and present, were a favorite topic.

That night, in the dark of the moon, a red '77 Ford pickup vanished from Scotchtown Farm. Had the name SCOTCHTOWN FARM stenciled on both doors in big letters. Folks suspected Peanut.

And two days later, we heard Peanut got himself surrounded down in Millboro Springs by dozens of officers from three counties, but Peanut slipped away that time, too.

A week later, they finally got him. He'd made it all the way up to Baltimore, Maryland. On the whole, we thought, he'd done better in the woods.

Anyway, Peanut, we hope you enjoyed your visit to Highland County as much as we did.

The Best Four Days in
Highland County

Every year, for four days in September, Highland County
has its county fair, the most important community event
of the year, a vital linking-up of country people, their
businesses, and skills.

I've become hesitant to mention the fair to city friends visiting at the time.

At first they're quite keen. It sounds like a really *neat* idea.
They'll promote it to their kids. "Carly, don't you want to see the
little lambs and the pigs and the pumpkins?"

But once on the fairgrounds, their enthusiasm wanes, and
they can scarcely conceal their yawns. One friend, a photographer
from Washington, D.C., walked through all the barns and exhibits
and never once unslung her camera. Another, a Princeton scientist,
met everybody I met: the sheepmen, the county supervisors, and
others. Hell, I thought he was having a good time. On the way
home, he said, "Now I see what the sociologists mean about in-
breeding."

I've never quite forgiven him for that.

Seen through city eyes, I admit, the fair isn't very impressive. The whole shebang—grandstand, barns, food booths, and midway —is tucked behind the high school, a one-story brick building on the outskirts of Monterey. What you can see from the parking lot won't make your heart beat faster. There are no hammer rides or death plunges, and the Ferris wheel is too small to scare a ten-year-old.

Local clubs run the food stands: the Bolar Ruritans, the Future Farmers of America (FFA), the Highland High School Band Boosters, and the Lions Club among them. A hand-lettered motto on the Monterey Methodist's booth says, EAT SO THE HUNGRY CAN EAT (the Methodists gave eleven hundred dollars to world hunger relief last year). Most booths are thirty-foot "single wides" with a serving window at one end. The McDowell Ladies' Auxiliary has a tent for the bingo game. They can play fifty cards at a time.

The midway is a single street of ring-tossing and balloon-bursting games with fuzzy-animal prizes in awful psychedelic colors. A child's merry-go-round, Ferris wheel, and two or three other rides are scattered about. Canned goods, flowers (single flowers and arrangements), sewing, hunting trophies, and arts and crafts cover long tables in the school gym, a cinder-block room dominated by a tremendous ram's head painted on the wall. The ram is blue and seems to be leering. Vegetables, hay bales, buckets of small grain (oats and buckwheat), and corn shocks go to the vegetable barn. The grandstand, in a pinch, might hold five hundred people.

That's the whole fair, except for the Highland County Library's quilt room (fifty cents admission) down the hall from the gym. Bernice Eubank borrowed the community's finest, rarest quilts to hang on the walls and drape on a couple of antique beds, and it's a grand display of colors and imagination. Women's art. Some of the quilters are alive and known to everybody, some are kin, some are not. The oldest quilt is dated 1847. It's a *Baltimore*

Album, assembled by a bride's family and friends. Most of the quilters used fruit- or flower-basket squares, but one artist made a more radical square: outsized moon, sun, stars, hex signs. Bernice had to beg the quilt's present owner (a devout Christian) to lend this beautiful pagan thing to the Highland County Fair.

Some women spend hours in this small brilliant room.

In the early twentieth century, county fairs were proving grounds for farm technologies, engines of a confident and expanding agriculture. Here, one found the newest machines and best-bred livestock, watched demonstrations by the state agricultural people, met drummers from John Deere and Cyrus McCormick.

Nowadays, the big fairs are diversions for our urban populace. The midways are enormous, with plenty of low-stakes gambling, and rock bands nightly. You can buy patented knife sharpeners or time-share condominiums on Bonzo Lake. The agricultural part of the fair is tucked away on the back lot.

Progressive American agriculture is in terrible disarray. Not so long ago, the American farm was hyped as an economic miracle where a single farmer could feed forty, fifty, or goodness knows how many hungry people. Remember "Food for Peace"?

This was the dream: The farmer would rise early in the morning and, after checking the futures on his computer, go into the farm factory, where he'd process food products all day. Like city people, he'd buy his own food from the supermarket, trade his car periodically, and take annual vacations. He'd live like the people on TV.

To finance this dream, the farmer leveraged his equity. He borrowed against his inherited farm to buy more land and bigger machines to work it. He was encouraged to do this by state agriculture schools, equipment makers, money lenders, and the United States government. "Plant fence line to fence line," he was told.

It wasn't a terrible dream, just a foolish one. But it had terrible consequences. It was the young, energetic, hard-working dreamers who failed. Farmer of the Year awards stood on the mantelpiece of many a bankrupt farm.

Most Highland County farmers are stubbornly conservative, deeply skeptical of advice from men who have something to sell and state-salaried PhD's who have nothing to lose when their advice goes wrong. Not many farms here net more than ten thousand dollars a year, but most are owned in fee simple. They boast large vegetable gardens, a few hogs, and some chickens scratching in the lane.

Recently, I was helping a neighbor round up a heifer who'd strayed in with Eldon Puffenbarger's cows. Eldon was weaning his calves at the time, milking his herd of twelve beef cattle by hand—that's how tame they were. Eldon's place is small but scrupulously kept. Thinking about the farm crisis, I asked the old man, "Eldon, I don't suppose you ever borrowed any money?"

Eldon demurred vigorously. "I did so," he said. "Back in 19 and 33 I borrowed five dollars to get married on." He paused to reflect. "Of course, five dollars was right smart money in 1933."

Highland County is waves of mountain ranges and plateaus. All the roads into the county are crooked, and you pay a fifty-dollar premium on a truckload of fertilizer if they have to haul it into Highland. It's high (the county fair is at three thousand feet), and livestock thrive in the cooler weather here. Industry amounts to one data processing plant and one sewing plant. You can't buy beer on Sundays or mixed drinks any time, but the state installed a liquor store in Monterey a few years back, over the objections of most of the citizens. Highland is bordered by the West Virginia counties of Pocohontas and Pendleton, and the Virginia counties of Augusta and Bath. Only Highland and Augusta still have county fairs, and Highland's is superior. In four nights, Wednesday through Saturday, the fair draws twenty thousand visitors— quite a crowd in a county of twenty-seven hundred citizens.

Many visitors at the fair were born here and return every

year to keep in touch. Some come from adjacent counties. Some hope to do a little business—sell a stud ram or replacement heifer, take orders for custom quilting, promote the basement taxidermy business. Some come to demonstrate skills, or to show what they're most proud of.

Me, I plan to run my young dog, Mack, at Saturday's sheep-dog trial. Mack is big for a Border Collie, quite powerful, and one day I might sell some of his pups. But first I want to have him competing against other working dogs, where everybody can get a good look at him. And I'm afraid Mack has some problems.

By saying city people are often bored by our county fair, I am not saying they're unwelcome. But, unlike the Fall Foliage Spectacular and the Maple Syrup Festival in spring, the fair isn't designed to attract tourist dollars. No attempt is made to tidy things up to fit the image urbanites have of us. If you're offended by the rows of deer trophies, you can look away. And if your idea of valid country life excludes the demolition derby, don't come to this fair on Thursday night.

Men roll logs into the horse arena to mark the combat zone, and the Monterey Fire Department slicks the dirt with tanker loads of water. Out back, behind the arc lights, young bucks tinker with their cars. Teams of kids try to ready their old clunker for one last run. One boy does his body work with the sharp edge of a splitting maul.

Shade-tree mechanics hover everywhere, in oily blue jeans, T-shirts, and gimmee caps so smudged you can't read the legends. Among the piston ring and camshaft set, these kids are hard core. And standing as near as they can get, hands in pockets, acting cool, the younger kids pray someone will ask them to find the 7/16ths socket or "put some water in that ———— radiator." One fourteen-year-old wears a T-shirt he's lettered HELL'S CHILDREN.

Although the drivers are seat-belted and helmeted, and the glass is out of the cars and you can't get up much steam on this small, slippery field, it must be lonely in the driver's seat moments before you and five others roar out to bash one another into immobility.

One car is labeled MAUD'S MASSAGE PARLOR. Another, in Darth Vader black, is THE MASTER OF DISASTER. Young bucks are fonder of racket than we older folks, and there's plenty of racket here. Over the bellowing engines the announcer shouts, "Number 14, you must hit a live car. A *live* car, Number 14!"

The smell is awful: burnt clutch, burnt rubber, antifreeze, blue oil smoke. The bitter stink of overheated engines makes me sneeze.

Our farm is thirty minutes from the nearest garage, double that to a shop that can adjust the timing on our hay baler. Many a Highland farm is more remote than ours. If it weren't for the shade-tree mechanics who make a poor living keeping our ancient machines alive for just one more season, what would we do? If their idea of fun is loudly demolishing the same vehicles they keep going the other 364 days in the year, there's not much a farmer can do but stick his fingers in his ears, grin, and bear it.

At the kiddy show, Friday afternoon, you don't see many young bucks. This crowd is women fourteen to one, with a high proportion of grandmothers. Pink seems a popular color. Blue, too. Our neighbor Mrs. Stephenson says, "When my Marylee was little, I brought her and she took third place." She sniffs. "I told Marylee her daughter'd be lucky to come in fourth!"

Prizes are awarded for healthiest baby, most charming, most appealing toddler, most attractive boy and girl, and (open to Highland residents only) Little Miss and Master Highland.

Rural counties are a bit like Ireland—beautiful to live in but a hell of a place to make a living. As in Ireland, the young emigrate. They leave here for the Shenandoah Valley, Richmond, or anywhere they can earn decent wages—enough, anyway, to raise a family. They always plan to return home one day. Maybe not this year. Next year, maybe.

There aren't a hundred eighteen kids *in* Highland County, but that's how many are entered today. The kids have come because they are the most important persons in their parents' lives, because Grannie begged they be brought here to show the home folks, right up onstage, in the spotlight, where they belong. The mothers dress casually, in spotless blue jeans and neat blouses, with perhaps a touch more makeup than usual. Most of the kids are uncertain, some are deeply shy. A few preen. I have to be in a particular frame of mind to enjoy the kiddy show, but the grandmothers all turn out.

Those who turn out for the sheep-dog trial are mostly livestock people, young and old. It is an undemanding audience. The poorest excuse of a stock dog gets applause from men who've hoofed after steers on a rampage or pursued young lambs through the tuckerbrush, cursing and breathless. I hope Mack won't be the poorest dog here, but he might be. Although Mack's a biddable (obedient) sheep dog, he has a savage grip (bite). He'll do the job if you keep him calm. Last spring, while sewing up a ewe that Mack bit, my wife suggested we rename him Stitches.

Winners at the sheep-dog trial and the kiddy show get ribbons. Some competitions give cash awards: first-place canned tomatoes, a dollar fifty; third-place art (junior, ages six to nine, acrylics), fifty cents. At the horse show, first prize in the keyhole race is twenty-five dollars (extra money added by Moyer's Arabians). Winner of the demolition derby takes one hundred dollars home. Best bear trophy or deer rack: five dollars.

A trophy hunter explained how to get a good timber rattlesnake without ruining the snakeskin with a bullet hole. "Stick him in your freezer, live, and shut the door," he said. "Next day you can mount him up nice."

The crafts judges form a sorority of expert peers, most from out of the county. Several have been to the judging school at the

Augusta Presbyterian Church, with cards to prove it. Unwary novice judges are assigned to cookies, jellies, and jams. Hundreds of sweet things are entered: platters of brownies, cakes, jams, and jellies. You'd think it would be fun tasting them, until you thought twice. The jelly judges did stay for lunch afterward (thanks to the Highland Girl Scouts), but they hardly ate a thing.

Sewing judges sit at a table while assistants bring them garments to inspect for fabric grain lines, stitching, suitable thread, smooth darts, pleats, tucks, gathers, and facings. One lady holds up a black-and-white-checked child's jumper. "Oh, look, she's covered the buttons."

The second judge turns a sundress pocket inside out to inspect the stitching. "What do you do when they're both nice?"

The senior judge says, "You get to nitpicking," and she awards first prize to the jumper. I don't know how it is in other places, but in Highland County, covered buttons are *it*.

Many skills and crafts shown here are traditional, but not all of them. Kids' art is pretty much the same as kids' art anywhere, a few more sheep and cows, a few less McDonald's arches. Mrs. Leo Schwartz has prepared a Japanese exhibit (Department E-2, Educational Exhibits) because an exchange student from Japan stayed with her family this summer. And Rafe Levien, a computer whiz, has an exhibit of computer art.

The canned-vegetable judges look for a perfect seal and a nice-looking ring and label. The liquid should be free of sediment and bubbles. The color should be natural, pieces must be uniform and of good quality. Mildred Detamore holds a jar of stewed tomatoes up to the light and sighs. "The tomatoes are so much seedier this year. It's because of the drought."

An assistant judge says, "Is that scorch in there? I believe she scorched them."

"No, that's too even for a scorch. She used pepper."

Next, they sort the green beans, discarding lesser entries until the top two stand side by side. Mildred says, "These beans are better sized. I like the younger beans. They're tenderer." In deference to the other jar (and its canner), she adds, politely, "I suppose some people like 'em more shelly," but firmly awards the younger beans first place.

The ladies judging quilts seem to have the most fun, perhaps because there is a bigger crew of them. But despite their laughter and cries of approval, they are awfully strict.

"You can see the backing through here and her corners don't quite meet. . . ."

"She's got a real imagination, but she didn't put enough quilting in it. She stopped too soon."

I don't know many men—myself included—who, judged by these ladies, would come off with a blue ribbon.

Dan Daughty, photo coordinator for the *Roanoke News,* is judging the photo contest. "Only a mother or father could do this," he says, eyeing one entry. The kid is two or three, with exploding blond hair, and a wall-to-wall grin. The focus is imperfect, and the lighting is standard frontal flash, but her grin . . .

"I have to give it first place," Daughty laughs. "Besides, it's a *tasteful* nude."

If you look quick at our fair, there's not much to it. But if you can slow your eye, you'll discover intensified moments in the ordinary fabric of life. You'll meet people famous locally: Virginia Swadley Rexrode, whose tatting and crocheting takes any awards her sister's work doesn't; Lewis Shumate, the archer; Sallie Kate Hammer, who, with her daughter, Karen Gutshall, has made the blue-ribbon quilt two years in a row (the judges could detect two different hands in the stitching, but didn't know which was whose); Buddy Hunt, the best sheep-dog trainer in Highland; and Mack Ratcliffe, who's ridden at the head of the fair parade for thirty years.

It rains all day Saturday and the arena is greasy mud. Highland has half a dozen serious horse breeders, perhaps five or six hundred horses, but horse people come to this show from all the counties around. In the announcer's booth I ask Mrs. Kincaid if the rain might force them to cancel. "Oh, no," she says. "We go right on ahead. They're grateful we don't cancel. Some of them have come an awful distance, and even if there's only one entered in a particular event, we hold it anyway."

In the keyhole race, from a jump start, horse and rider hurl themselves to the far end of the arena, brake, pivot, race back to the start. In dry weather, the keyhole race is one thing. In wet, it's yellow slickers flying and mud clots kicked up and hanging in the air, and when four horse legs brake in that mud, the horse goes down on his haunches, and the slightest miscalculation by horse or rider could snap a leg like a matchstick.

Earlier that afternoon, when I walked onto the sheep-dog trial course with my dog, Mack, it was already raining. I kept one eye on the three sheep at the top of the course and another on Mack, who wore a puzzled expression. "What's that, boss? What kind of work are we doing today?" With a nervy dog you've got to pretend to be calm when you don't feel it. Relax. You've got to go easy with your commands, voice, or whistles.

The judge watched the whole thing from the front seat of a one-ton pickup, with the windshield wipers going.

Unless you have an unseemly addiction to ring toss, it's hard to spend much money at the fair. A season ticket (including all grandstand events) is $7.50. A foot-long hot dog (with chili) from the Highland High School Band Boosters is $1.50; and a country ham sandwich from the Bolar Ruritans is the same. Funnel cakes are $1.25. But the pièce de résistance is served Friday and Saturday nights when the Ruritans fire up their barbecue pit. The Ruritans' chicken dinner (half a chicken, French fries, coleslaw, and roll) is $4.50 and well worth it. This year, the French fries were unsalted, so I assume some of the Ruritans have high blood pressure like I do.

The fair brags that it has "The Best Sheep Show in Virginia," and since Virginia is the biggest sheep state on the East Coast, that's no modest boast. Friday afternoon they hold the adult live-stock show and you will see some fine animals then, but the morning 4-H show probably draws more people. Two or three hundred stand around as the kids bring steers, heifers, lambs, rams, and brood ewes into the ring behind the livestock barn. Usually their animals started out in their parents' flock or herd, but some of the older kids bought fancier animals with this show in mind. They've done the routine feeding, grooming, and vet care for six months to a year. Today their animals will be judged and sold. The youngest kids are six; they graduate into the FFA at thirteen or so. Boys barely outnumber girls.

It's clear that the experience teaches kids, and the lessons they learn are far from simple.

Bill Bratton, farmer and volunteer fireman, works for the Soil Conservation Service. He's come to the 4-H show to help out but can't do much because a ruptured disc forces him to spend most of his time sitting. The first time Bill Bratton showed a steer he was younger than his daughter Shawna (who will capture first prize today). "I'd picked a calf out from my daddy's herd and fed it out myself. When they get some size on them, they can eat twenty-five pounds of feed a day. I thought the world of that steer, but when we took him to the show—it was in Roanoke and they were showing twenty-seven steers that day—the state grader looked him over and said no, I hadn't made the cut. I couldn't show him. Now, that was one heartbroken little boy. Lester Dalton—he was extension agent then—Lester stepped in. Lester said, 'This boy has come all the way here to show his steer and by God, he's going to show it. I don't care if he's dead last, he's going to show it.' I showed the steer. I wasn't dead last, either. I was two up from last. I'll never forget that."

After the orphan lamb class, where the youngest kids com-pete and every single kid gets a blue ribbon, the judge settles down to some serious judging. The kids lead their market steers into the ring, where the judge waits with the county agent and the high-school vocational-agriculture teacher. Each kid stands his animal, walks it, arranges it in the ranking the judge dictates. Curry combs sticking out of the back pockets of their jeans, one-hundred-pound girls restrain fourteen-hundred-pound cattle. The kids betray no expression even when they momentarily lose control and an adult has to grab for the halter to help settle the animal down.

The judge, Dennis Smith, is from Broadway, Virginia. Once he has the steers lined up to his satisfaction, he takes up the microphone and the kids stand still as he tells the whole world what he thinks.

"Now, this first-place steer is a high-yielding steer, maybe a little too heavy. . . .

"This next steer is carrying plenty of condition for today's market, and I might have placed him higher if he'd showed more expression of muscle. . . ."

The judge is deliberate and rather formal. When he finds fault with an animal, his criticism is courteous. "Now, this is a more old-fashioned type of animal, and he just doesn't have the capacity I'd like to see. . . ."

In a daze, Amy Halterman leads a light heifer around the ring, the lead strap wrapped tightly around her wrist. If that calf took a notion to bolt, she'd snatch young Amy right with her, but grown-up eyes are on her, watching out for the child. Amy is told that the heifer is hers to keep. "Can I keep her in my room?" she asks.

For the very young kids—Amy, the children with their cute beribboned orphan lambs—there's room for sentiment. The older kids know better. The animals they've befriended and cared for in the bitterest weather go on the block tonight and to slaughter not long afterward; and the judge isn't discussing the animal's qualities *qua* animal, he's judging meat. When he runs his hand down a lamb's back, he's feeling for chops. When he talks about a steer's muscling, he doesn't mean physique, he means rump roast and steaks.

So what do these kids learn? Some learn the difference between love and knowledge. Undoubtedly, some will learn that their parents' chosen breed of sheep or cattle isn't much admired by other grown-ups in the community.

Today, as every day, some who don't deserve to will win, and some will lose. Older kids have tricks that younger kids will have to learn: Good showmanship can conceal defects from the most critical eye. Some kids, who didn't sleep very well last night, will learn that things rarely go as bad as our worst fears, or as well as our brightest hopes.

Just a month ago, little Terry Turner's fine market lamb took to eating maple leaves. Nothing is wrong with that, but the lamb stuck her head into a hornets' nest and was stung horribly. Everybody did what they could, but the lamb's neck swelled shut and she died. Terry's grandfather found him another to show, but it wasn't good as the first and placed seventh in its class.

So some learn about bad luck. But there is unexpected kindness in this world, too, and most people wish you well, most of the time.

Today, a yearling steer will bring fifty-eight to sixty-one cents a pound at the livestock market. If you bucket-feed a single animal for the 4-H show, you'll have more money than that in him by the time you sell.

On a rainy Saturday night, under the tent set up for this purpose, one at a time, high to low, the kids bring out their animals to sell. A good crowd of bidders watches: farmers, businessmen, Delbert Rexrode from the First and Citizens Bank. Most everybody wears raingear and rubber boots. Plastic covers the auctioneer's Stetson.

Buddy Hunt sells me a 4-H raffle ticket. They're going pretty well, he says. Second prize is a wool blanket. First is a Border Collie pup.

It's a real auction and farmers note prices in their auction sheets the same as they always do, but the steer prices start at sixty-eight cents and go up from there. "Seventy-three, seventy-three, give four, four, four. *Sold* to Hevener Motor Equipment of Franklin, West Virginia. That's the home of John Deere. Thank you for coming out tonight."

These men have come out in a pouring rain to pay far too much for animals they don't need or want, so the 4-H kids will get a little something for their work, so they will do the same perhaps for the next generation.

The First and Citizens Bank buys the champion steer. Monterey Livestock and Jack Bauserman Livestock jointly bid in the champion lamb at three dollars a pound. It's a cheerful occasion, and many awful jokes are told as normally thrifty farmers bid 'em up.

The 4-H auction is a success, and the 4-H raffle brings in two hundred fifty dollars—enough so all the 4-H kids can rent a bus and go to Richmond for the Virginia State Fair. I doubt they'll like the state fair as well as their own, but they're excited about it.

Saturday, near noon, my young dog ran his very first sheepdog trial. Mack came in third. Now, you mightn't think it's a high honor coming in third in a class of three, but I was proud of him. I fastened his yellow ribbon right to his collar. A couple of sheepdog people complimented him. He did an honest job of work and, despite my fears, he didn't bite his sheep.

Faith

One gray Sunday afternoon, last September, I was coming down from Scotland on the train. Though I had a Britrail pass, I'd only twenty pounds in my pocket and London's no town to arrive in at dark, no hotel room, not much money, so I jumped off the train in York. I wandered the crooked peculiar streets of that medieval town looking for a cheap place to sleep. It was dusk. Behind the lighted windows of the stone churches came the notes of evensong.

York Minster Cathedral is a great gray pile, wonderful and hideous all at once. How do they heat it in the wintertime? York Minster seems too grand and too austere for the contents of any one religion. It is a testament to faith.

People are buried under the floors: bishops, clerics, soldiers, prominent women and men. Their epitaphs are hard to read. Feet have trod the stone letters smooth.

There aren't many visitors so late.

In the alcove, I happened across a clumsily sculpted, crudely painted statue of a knight who'd died three hundred years ago. PAUSE YE PILGRIM THAT YOU MAY READ THIS MESSAGE FROM YE DEAD.

I paused.

Apparently this knight was a good man, beloved of his friends, respected even by his enemies. He was easy with the powerful, gentle with the poor, valued in his community. He had wealth, but not a crippling amount of it. His children lived to be well married. His wife was constant to the end. PILGRIM, HE HAD ALL THESE THINGS AND YET HE DIED.

In York Minster Cathedral, the feet of the faithful grooved these stone steps, blurred the granite epitaphs of great men; faith is harder than stone.

I grew up attending a little Lutheran church out in Montana. Oliver Jones, pastor of that church, visited the sick and elderly, the infirm, those in need. On Sundays, he'd stand up and talk about his faith. Unlike Jim Bakker and Jimmy Swaggart, he wasn't a good speaker. Oliver Jones was too honest. Oh, he'd be going along just fine and then he'd remember some qualification, some purely human difficulty, and he'd pause to note that and lose his thread, and I was a teenager sitting in the very back of that church, just aching to get out of there.

Years later, on the other coast of the country, when I'm in difficulties, I find myself thinking about Pastor Oliver Jones, wondering what he would have done. I don't have much faith. All our lives are shaped by the faith of others.

PART V

The Land
Stewards

Helen

Nearing

It didn't used to be this way.

In 1971, when Anne and I moved to our Appalachian farm, we were ignorant of rural living until our new neighbors educated us. Farms on either side were active, and along our valley, vigorous men and women planted oats and corn, made hay, gardened, and kept hogs and sheep, horses and cattle. We few urban expatriates swapped equipment, helped one another during hay season, and got together for picnics or to pick apples for cider. There were fourteen working farms along our road.

Today, nobody raises hogs. We're the only ones who still bother with the cider. Only old Gene Mitchel plants oats. Most of the farms have been leased to out-of-country stockmen, or have grown up in cedars, or have been broken up for summer homes and hunting camps. Including ours, there are just four farms left.

The urban expatriates mostly returned to the city and suburbs. Those who stayed we see every year at the county fair and say how we really ought to get together more often. We're too far apart to share equipment.

It began to make me wonder. Farming has always been hard work and, unless you exploit your soil or livestock, spectacularly unremunerative. Most of the friends we left behind in the city are doing pretty well and many have weekend country places now. Probably someone like me keeps an eye on the properties and runs a brush hog over the weeds before the owners come out Memorial Day to begin their season.

Last fall, Anne and I had a bad lambing, and almost as soon as it was done, road hunters shot and killed two of our ewes—for the hell of it, I guess. The wee lambs were banked against their dead mothers when we found them.

So. It was time to talk to some people wiser than myself about what was going on in the American countryside. If I couldn't find new answers, perhaps I could revive the old ones. I'd ask those wise men and women about land and work, community, food, and money. But beneath these queries I had a personal question of my own:

Should we sell the farm?

Late May, pale delicate birch leaves were shivering in the spring wind of Penobscot Bay, Maine. Here, so far north, the apple trees were just blooming. The forest was scrubby third-growth spruce, with scattered houses built practically on the state highway so snowplows could dig them out in the wintertime. The houses looked hard-used and many bore FOR SALE signs. The grange hall at the crossroads looked abandoned.

This is rumpled, glaciated country. Some of the few remaining working farms had burnt off their fields, and the first plants to poke through the harsh black stubble were the tenderest ferns.

I'd never met Helen Nearing but had heard plenty about her. In the 1960s, near the height of the back-to-the-land movement, dozens of my friends had made this pilgrimage to the Nearings'

Forest Farm. These young people hoped to emulate the home-steading life the Nearings had lived since, well, since before most of us were born.

In 1932, Scott and Helen Nearing left New York for a down-at-the-heels Vermont farm. There they grew their own food, cut their own wood (by hand—Scott Nearing hated the noise of a chain saw), and devised a method of stone-concrete construction (*slipform*, they called it) to build a fine house, sugarhouse, and several studios. For cash, they sugared. The Nearings wrote and published dozens of political tracts, but it was *Living the Good Life,* their 1954 homesteading autobiography, that influenced a later generation. It sat on every homesteader's bookshelf, right between *Trout Fishing in America* and *Raising Goats the Modern Way.*

In 1952 the Nearings moved to Maine, where Scott died in 1984. But Helen is still vigorous, still homesteading, still receiving visitors.

I turned left at Harborside, just like the local postmistress had instructed. She'd been polite but reserved, like she'd given these directions too many times before.

Forest Farm perches above the dark rocks of Spirit Cove, a small inlet that's just a notch in the greater Penobscot. The mail-box bears no name, but when I pulled up beside a substantial stone workshop, a roughly hand-lettered wooden sign advised HELP US LIVE THE GOOD LIFE: VISITORS 3–5.

Helen had been lying out on a patio bench, getting a bit of rare Maine spring sunshine when I arrived. Immediately she jumped up and hurried inside the house (the Nearings, as paragons of industry, wouldn't be caught snoozing in the sun).

The Nearing house is neat but not as grand as it looks from photographs in the *Good Life* books. A steep roof and dark wooden balconies, front and back, give the place a Tyrolean effect. Slipform stonework resembles white chocolate with an overabundance of nuts. Most houses in this part of Maine are wood framed, mostly white Cape Cods. The Nearings' home owes nothing to vernacular architecture. It is exactly what the Nearings wanted; just that, and no apologies.

Helen came back outside, ready now to talk. Her skin was deeply lined, but her eyes were as clear as a young girl's. Although I knew she was eighty-five, she looked to be about sixty. She wore a tan, hand-knitted sweater bought at a garage sale. The sweater had a black cat on the front, and as we talked, she tugged at its silly yarn tail. We sat on the wooden bench side by side, and on that lovely spring afternoon she put me at ease. We talked about the spring; how different the gardening season is so far north.

We moderns speak quickly, in snappy sentences. Helen speaks in much longer sentences with subordinate clauses which, taken together, create paragraphs that express her meanings with no ambiguity. It is the speech pattern of an earlier era and of a much more rational mind.

"We didn't come to the country for any high moral purpose, you know," she explained. "It was America turned Scott into a radical. In a better society he would have been a conservative."

In the movie *Reds,* Scott is one of the witnesses—real people who actually knew the film's protagonists, John Reed and Louise Bryant. The witnesses are contradictory, elderly, confused. Scott is merely uncooperative. "No," he says, "I'm not going to talk about people, no sir. I'm not a purveyor of neighborhood gossip or anything of the kind. That's not my job." That was Scott. Although the movie studio promised to pay Guild minimum to the witnesses, it never paid Scott a dime. That was typical, too.

In 1915, Scott was fired as an economics professor at the University of Pennsylvania for opposing child labor. In 1919, he was tried under the Espionage Act for writing "The Great Madness," an antiwar pamphlet. From the witness stand an unrepentant Scott said, "To my mind the great curse of war is that it is built on fear and hate." He was acquitted.

Scott debated with Bertrand Russell and Clarence Darrow

and ran for Congress against New York Mayor Fiorello La-Guardia. When he broke with the Communist Party, the Communists consigned him and his writings to "the scrap heap of the revolution." In 1928, when Helen met Scott, he was unemployed and unemployable, widely published, but no longer publishable. Sixty years afterward, Helen recalls almost dreamily how she recognized Scott's qualities at once. He had "a sincerity, a purpose, an integrity. The first hour or two I sized him up and I think he sized me up."

When Helen took up with Scott, they were as poor as they could get. Huddled in their freezing apartment on New York's Avenue C, they sought a better way. Being poor in the country is easier than being poor in the city, they decided, and so they spent three hundred dollars for a down payment on a run-down Vermont farm. There, at least, they could grow their own food.

The Nearings worked. How they worked. They were strict vegetarians, teetotalers, nonsmokers. Their pleasures were long walks, music (Helen was a trained musician), and each other's company. Scott continued to write nonstop, producing thirteen pamphlets between 1934 and 1954. They included *Democracy Is Not Enough* and *The New World Order and Some of its Immediate Problems,* among others. His books didn't make the best-seller lists.

In 1954, Scott and Helen wrote *Living the Good Life (How to Live Sanely and Simply in a Troubled World)*. They published it themselves and the book disappeared. In 1970, when it was republished by Shocken Books, *Living the Good Life* sold 170,000 copies. Although Scott never stopped writing his political tracts, it was the *Good Life* books that people read: *The Good Life Album* (1974), *Continuing the Good Life* (1979), *Wise Words for the Good Life* (1980), *Our Home Made of Stone: Building in our Seventies and Nineties* (1987), even a cookbook—*Simple Food for the Good Life* (1985).

By 1952, the countryside around their Vermont farm had changed, with skiers and summer people in droves. The Nearings decided to move to Maine. Because Scott didn't believe in profits, they deeded most of their seven-hundred-acre Vermont farm to the town of Winhall as a nature preserve and sold the remainder for only the cash and labor they'd put into it. They took fifteen thousand dollars for property appraised at four times that amount.

Scott was funny about money. He refused inheritances and gifts that would have made him wealthy. "The only thing more cowardly than a million dollars," Scott liked to say, "is two million dollars."

On Maine's Penobscot Bay, the Nearings began again. When they started their new home, Helen was in her seventies and Scott was ninety.

One year Helen ticked visitors on her calendar, counting twenty-three hundred of them. This year she expected there would only be a thousand or so. She has built a modest shelter for her visitors. "Look, it's a mushroom house," she said, and indeed, the unpainted slat-sided wooden structure does look like a mushroom. "They can stay here and I show them the pump and the outhouse, and when they come to the house, I'll feed them."

She showed me around her homestead. There's a fifty-by-fifty-foot walled garden where she grows marigolds and other flowers for color as well as the vegetables Scott preferred. Behind the garden are deep rectangular compost bins. Cleaned, oiled garden tools lean against the back wall of the stone greenhouse. Inside the greenhouse, among the lettuces and spinach, is a great volunteer poppy. "I don't know where that came from," she said, patting the pod like it was a furry, tiny baby. "Perhaps God sent it.

"When Scott saw the soil here, he didn't think we could garden at all." She handed me a chunk of hard white stuff. "It's all clay. I think you could pot with it."

The good earth the Nearings created is springy under my feet from years of soil building with compost.

The living room is lined, ceiling to floor, with books: classics, novels by Hardy and Tolstoy, and others. There is no television set. In the evenings, she and Scott would talk or read to each other.

Helen reads science fiction, too—Bradbury, Arthur C. Clarke—and a shelf holds her anti-Shakespeare books. "He never wrote the plays," Helen confided. I smiled, pleased to see any human goofiness among the sort of order and rationality I admire in her but could never emulate.

The workshop is orderly, with neatly labeled jars of screws and a splendid wooden tool chest (oak? elm? beechwood?) whose drawers are lined with sharp long wood bits. "They were Scott's grandfather's," she said. "Just as good as new."

When Helen slid the drawer shut, she enclosed a bit of history and a different way of looking at things. Those bits were made in a time when tools might outlast their owner.

Helen has written about gathering stones that she and Scott used for building. "From the birth of our idea of building a stone house, we started collecting these rocks. From roadsides, from our garden, gravel pit, old stone walls, on walks in the woods, all over the countryside we kept our eyes open for well-shaped rocks of any cartable size."

Helen pointed out a new pile of building stones. "There," she said, "that stone's a good corner." She's eighty-five, and doesn't have more building in mind. But habits of a lifetime . . .

Even when in his nineties, Scott wheeled stones and mixed cement. He dug out a farm pond by hand: fifteen thousand wheelbarrows full of muck. When I looked through the family album, there weren't many snapshots of Scott sitting still. He's a wizened, ancient man, hoeing, sawing, trundling a wheelbarrow; Scott cut wood by hand until he was ninety-eight. Helen looked at her woodpile. "I have to buy it now, alas."

Her hands were rough, lined, puffy, the way hands get after a lifetime of manual labor. Her fingernails were crooked, broken. When she caught me staring, she said, "I was trained as a violinist, you know. I was twenty-six before I planted so much as a radish. Oh, I was lily-handed."

The average American family today has about the same buying power it had in the mid-1960s, but today it takes two wage earners to provide the income once provided by one. That's seventy to eighty work hours per family per week. The Nearings divided their days exactly: four hours for bread labor (tending their garden, making their cash living); four hours for reading, study, and writing; and four for social activities. Sundays they did no bread labor. In the winter months, the Nearings often traveled, visiting socialists and vegetarians in China, Japan, Europe, and Ceylon.

The Nearings refused to keep animals (except cats) and were strict vegetarians. Scott's idea of a gourmet dinner was garden beans, a potato, and some applesauce. This produced several effects, some not readily predictable. Because they had no livestock, they didn't need machines to make winter fodder, so they had no baler, mower, or tractor. They preferred simple hand tools. Helen does have a freezer, a water pump, and a car. The washer and dryer somebody gave her is still in the basement, never hooked up.

As a nonvegetarian who raises meat animals, I am skeptical of vegetarian health claims but, in fairness, note that Scott was a hundred when he died; and last year, when Helen found herself locked out on her balcony, she hang-dropped twelve feet to the cobblestones below, unharmed—an athletic feat for a woman half her age.

Because they kept their expenses low (the modern *necessities* they didn't own makes a long list), their income was modest—and in an America generally hostile to radical ideas, this financial independence kept them fearless.

The Nearings' true community was a political one: friends like Pete Seeger and Studs Terkel, and the homesteading apprentices who came to learn and stayed for a time. When I asked

Helen what regrets she had about their homesteading experience, she sighed and said, "Our failure to make headway with our neighbors in Vermont."

Most of the Nearings' attempts at rural cooperation failed. They thought the Vermonters were undisciplined. The Vermonters, in turn, thought anyone who ate vegetables out of a wooden bowl was peculiar. Their Vermont neighbors' comments are quoted at length in the Nearings' FBI file.

In an odd way, the Nearings were lucky. Their homesteading experiment was insulated from the social disruption of dying farm communities.

These days, Penobscot Bay is in the midst of a development boom of summer homes and vacation condos. Just down the road from Forest Farm, eight acres of waterfront land sold recently for two hundred thousand dollars. Helen Nearing shook her head. "There's no hiding place anymore," she said.

The next day when I stopped to say good-bye, Helen was making pea trellises. Her pea plants had responded to a morning watering with two inches of new growth, and Helen took a child's delight in the green, growing things. It was as if these were the first pea plants she had ever seen.

As we spoke, she knotted twine together, her hands busy, and she asked me about my farm. She said that when she lived in the mountains, she always wanted to be by the sea, but now she likes to go back to the mountains. She laughed.

She gets letters all the time from 1960s homesteaders who are still at it. "I am pleasantly surprised at the caliber of the young people who come here today and are willing to try. They are more serious—they know some of the difficulties."

When I asked her about the future of homesteading, she shrugged and said, "As the world gets worse, maybe homesteading will get a better aspect to it."

Her eyes brightened when she started talking about her grandson-in-law Peter Schumann, who heads the Bread and Pup-

pet Theatre, a political-minded theater troupe/festival in Vermont.
(She gave her violin to Peter when she stopped playing a few years
ago.) Every summer Bread and Puppet has a free concert near
Stratton, Vermont, and every year Helen is there. "Peter bakes the
bread and I slice and serve it." She laughed. "I'm afraid it isn't
particularly good bread. The show is free and the bread is free."
She showed me the scrapbooks, pictures, and articles of the tremendous monster puppets the theater uses to play out its political
parables. "You have to see it. Perhaps you could write about it."

Helen is working on another *Good Life* book. *Leaving the
Good Life,* it's called. "How to exit gracefully."

Oh.

She looked around the home she and Scott had built, the
lifestyle they'd so deliberately constructed. "I would like to end
here. This place is my shell, my skin. I shall stay here as long as I
can."

She smiled. She said another visitor was due at Forest Farm
that afternoon. She said, "I think I'll fix her a potato."

I said good-bye and offered my hand. She looked at me. "We
did this because we had to. One of the reasons we continued doing
it was that it showed people who were kicked out of society how
to survive." She ignored my hand and gave me a great big moth-
erly hug.

Helen Nearing was right. The hug was better.

Wendell

Berry

Twenty years ago, when I first met Wendell Barry, I'd never lambed a ewe, never baled hay, never changed a spark plug. But I was going to the country to be a home-steader. Dear God.

My wife and I were crisscrossing the southern Appalachians looking for land: a farm with good water, deep meadows, and big trees. We hadn't a clue how rare such places were. I'd hammered together a wood and canvas camper, the Gazebo, for the back of our bright red pickup truck, and it stayed dry as long as it didn't rain. The inside was snug, with a cook shelf, Coleman stove, kerosene lamp, and bedding. An apple-crate bookcase held tat-tered copies of *The Whole Earth Catalog* and Wendell Berry's essays and poems. You might recall that moment in our history when books were tools.

Wendell Berry and his wife, Tanya, were startled and not altogether pleased by our unannounced, uninvited arrival, but they put a courteous face on it. Wendell showed me his farm; the studio he'd built; the eroded hillside he was renovating. He pointed to bathtub-deep gullies and hard patches of bare subsoil; showed me where he'd sowed fescue and planted black walnut seedlings to stabilize the soil. ("Fescue," I wrote in my notebook.)

Tanya fed us a chicken dinner. I asked Wendell where we should look for a farm. If he were free to move, he said, he'd look in the mountains of western Virginia.

Free to move?

Wendell said a developer had bought a parcel of land right next door. The man planned to erect and sell dozens of tacky weekend camps. Although deeply upset, Wendell was going to stay put. He was a Kentuckian, and this bit of Kentucky was his place. "It's been one of our worst faults as a people," he said. "When things got difficult, we've always moved on."

Ignorance alters the landscape. Twenty years ago, on that first drive through Henry County, Kentucky, I'd thought it homely and inhospitable. Of course, I was scared: I was a New Yorker, and this was the South. America had been divided in twain by war and protest, and I feared this wasn't my side of the twain: too many rifles in pickup truck racks, too many American flags on windshields.

Now it's early summer 1989, and Henry County is lovely. After a night's heavy rain the air is washed, and beside the road, pale, bulbous tobacco plants shimmer. Spikes shoot up, stiff with pink and white flowers. The creeks run heavy and brown and tree scraps have been beaten onto the road. On the high plateau, near the wonderfully named town of Pleasureville, the farms are particularly prosperous, well tended, neat. There are dairy farms and beef farms. Sheep and goats browse next to faded black tobacco barns.

I'm not in a hurry and I want to see how this countryside matches the fictional Port William community of Berry's novels and stories. I am hoping to find the hotel where Jack Beecham ended his days (in *The Memory of Old Jack*).

Older houses in Port Royal, Kentucky, have steeply pitched roofs and broad front porches. In a front yard a fawn grazes, tied by a rope.

The farming infrastructure is still intact in Henry County, but along the hillsides above the Kentucky River, men have retreated from their steeper ground. You can still pick out the fields, but they are giving way to desolate patches of briars and thistles.

Approaching from the south, there's just one hill pasture, green as good bottomland, defiantly lush, high above the invisible line below which everybody else has withdrawn. That field belongs to Lane's Landing Farm, Berry's place. His drive is bordered by apple trees.

Berry is a lanky man with a Kentuckian's slow courtesy and thoughtful speech. He apologizes that Tanya can't be here today (family obligations).

> As I slowly fill with the knowledge of this place and sink into it, I come to the sense that my life here is inexhaustible, that its possibilities lie rich behind and ahead of me, that when I am dead it will not be used up.
> —*The Long-Legged House,* 1969

We amble along the hillside that the developer had bought so many years ago. His project had collapsed, and Berry now owns the land. "He planned to put sixty camps here. No sewage nor running water." Today the hillside is newly mown pasture, with bluegrass making an appearance among the fescue Barry has sown.

Whenever practicable, Berry farms with horses. When he brings out his palamino-colored Belgian geldings, it is done with evident pleasure. "I suppose I should have saved the best for last," he says, giving one of the great beasts a pat.

I don't believe his steeper ground could be farmed by a tractor, and I think some of his swaths would be dangerous to work even behind a horse. "You can stock this hillside and pasture it forever," he says. "The limiting factor is the human."

From interstates, at sixty-five mph, most American farms look OK. But on foot, bending over the dead soil, clambering through the gullies, a man begins to see problems. Some Iowa farms lose a bushel of topsoil for every bushel of corn they produce.

Kentucky hill farms erode quickly and repairs are slow and difficult to achieve. Some cleverness is required as well. Berry moved one hill gate when he noticed that his milk cows, hurrying downslope for feed, would brake at that spot and their hoofs, digging for purchase, were stripping the soil.

In the woods bordering his hill pastures, Berry thins the saplings, leaving the promising timber trees. Afterward he grazes sheep in the openings. As in all good farming, the input is simple —it's the thinking that's complex.

The costs: Berry's labor, chain-saw upkeep, maintenance of the horses who drag his felled trees to exactly where he wants them. The benefits: firewood, fence posts, erosion control (he fills hillside gullies with limbs and tops), and horse training.

After the sheep graze the brush away, grass is oversown. The results are a two-story agriculture of good pasture and valuable timber. Other predictable effects are less measurable: Berry's own good health and the rich tilth of the soil these practices develop.

Contrast these methods with one common practice of industrial agriculture. When an agribusinessman hires an expensive crop duster to spray for alfalfa weevils, he may increase this year's alfalfa production. He may also kill his neighbor's bees and his own earthworms and beneficial insects. He may pollute well-water downslope from his fields. If he is not very careful, he will do all these things.

Simplicity is the most beguiling promise of industrial agriculture, but its simplicity comes only by disguising inevitable effects as side effects and pretending that complex machines never cause problems. What's simple about a crop-dusting airplane?

> We might make a long list of things that we would have to
> describe as primary values . . . the one with which we have
> the most intimate working relationship is the topsoil.
>
> —*Home Economics,* 1987

Berry's lambs fatten on alfalfa. His riverside field has deep shade at the verges and clean water for the lambs to drink. He uses high-tensile, electrified permanent fencing and a good bit of portable electric fencing, too. These Cheviot lambs are big, nicely muscled and bloomy—as fine as any I've seen outside a show ring. Cheviots originated in high country, and I'm surprised to see them thriving in such a humid, close climate.

Over the years, Berry has added to his original place and now has a hundred and twenty-five acres. He jokes that he has six deeds to his farm. The woods above the lamb pasture belong to the most recent addition and untreated gullies here are leg breakers.

For many years Kentucky farmers practiced what Berry calls slash-and-burn agriculture. They'd clear and burn the trees, plow a tobacco patch, and let the land revert to woods when fertility failed. Forty years later, they'd repeat the process.

We pass a cord of firewood and gullies Berry has begun to fill. It's hot in the woods, and when we come out onto hill pasture again, the grass is almost too thick to walk through. New grass is closing a bulldozer scar. Berry bends to show me an unusual purple flowering lespedeza. Before we go on, he opens his pen knife to snip the only thistle in sight.

When Berry left a New York university two decades ago and returned to the country where he'd grown up, friends warned him about endangering his career; about what they saw as the inevitable stupefaction of farm life. Berry farmed, taught, and wrote such works as *The Memory of Old Jack* and *A Place on Earth* (novels); *The Unsettling of America* and *The Gift of Good Land* (essays); *The Country of Marriage* and *Sabbaths* (poetry). His books were well regarded, but set no sales records. I believe his readers were mostly country people.

> Like the water / of a deep stream, love is always too much. / We did not make it. Though we drink till we burst / we cannot have it all, or want it all. / In its abundance it survives our thirst. / In the evening we come down to the shore /to drink our fill, and sleep, while it / flows through the regions of the dark.
>
> —*The Country of Marriage,* 1973

We talk of America's attitudes toward farmers. I ask Berry why urban people picture farmers in such extremes: either as honest toilers of the soil, more moral and earthy than the rest of us, or as rubes, hayseeds, or hicks.

Berry grew up knowing good farmers. "There were very few tractors here until the late forties," he told me. "The old farming lasted here partly because of the demand for quality tobacco, which required plenty of hard work and plenty of knowledge, too. I grew up among people who were committed to farming. They spoke of a 'good un'—good crops, good animals. They'd say of a horse, 'He isn't much now, but he was a good un in his day.' They liked good judgment in a man. I knew what a 'good un' was and liked it.

"I'm not talking about nostalgia. I don't think the world can live without this. The question is: What does the land require to remain productive?

"Tobacco work was the hardest sort of work and these people cherished conversation. Somebody'd tell a joke early, establish a theme, somebody else would embellish it, and it'd go on like that all day.

"And there was great eating back in those days. Did you ever hear the expression 'I've ate after her'?" He laughs. " 'I've ate after a lot of women in my life, but she was the best.' "

These were the little luxuries around the edge of the difficult.

"When I came back to Henry County at thirty," Berry says, "I'd seen a bit of the world. Farming was getting worse and communities were breaking apart. I had been trying to find out what was going on. The rural sociologists, without exception, thought farmers needed better things than groveling in the earth. They thought that once rural people got out there where the lights were bright, they'd never return. The economy threw people's rural values against urban and industrial values."

It is pleasant on Berry's porch. Birds sing in the trees beside the deep brown river. Berry cherishes small farming, farming that attends to agricultural rules rather than industrial rules. I ask if there are any good farmers left.

"The Amish," he says quickly. "Perhaps the Mormons—I don't know. I haven't been out to see them." He notes that Pennsylvania's Lancaster County, worked in small tracts (eighty acres or so) by Amish farmers using only horses, is one of the most productive agricultural counties in America. "David Kline [an Amish farmer] doesn't count cultivation as an expense because he likes it so much. Labor is what a farmer has to market. Not technology. Technology is intelligence externalized and put into the service of others. If I want the benefit of my thought, I've got to do it with my head."

He tells about Lancie Clippenger, a farmer who turns farrowing sows onto pasture to pig. "They've got plenty of shade and water," Clippenger had told him, "and I see them every day." The man was using nature, investing not in the expansive, complex farrowing houses of modern agribusiness, but investing instead in pigs. His costs were low, the major inputs being his intelligence and attention.

But why was the American farmer so helpless before the forces that seemed to be destroying him? Why were Iowa children suffering from malnutrition?

Berry sighs. "The experts have been advising them they can't afford to raise their own food. Remember that Willie Nelson thing [Farm Aid]? A lot of that money went to buy food for farmers."

Farmers have fought environmentalists, animal-rights people, and conservationists. "They haven't made many friends," Berry says. "They've identified with their oppressors."

Sitting on his porch on a drowsy afternoon, I think how rural Kentucky has grounded Berry. For most Americans, communities are merely communities of interest or occupation. Years ago, when so many marched against the Vietnam War, it cost only inconvenience, but when Wendell Berry spoke out on this matter in 1968, he began, "I am a Kentuckian by birth, by predilection, and by choice. There are a good many people in this state I love deeply. And of those perhaps only four believe that I should be speaking here today, and one of them is me. If that defines the difficulty of this speech, it also defines the necessity."

The importance of speaking out depends on where you speak out from.

In Kentucky, however, as in the rest of America, rural communities are dying and the working landscape is changing. At best, farms become recreation homes for urbanites who think, maybe, someday, that's where they'd like to go to retire.

"They think it's restful in the country," Berry says. "They think you can buy a farm and go out on the weekends and rest. Many of them become terribly disillusioned. If I were a city person and wanted to buy a farm, I wouldn't live on the farm, I wouldn't plant a crop, no livestock. I'd just grass it down and mow it. I'd pay for it out of my salary. Just sit tight until it was mine."

I know few people who haven't yearned for simplicity. At the close of his long life, Scott Nearing's desire was to leave the world with nothing—no money, nothing. Like Ghandi, he wanted to leave only a dhoti and a pair of spectacles behind.

But although souls may be simple, places never are. Country places least of all.

"The human community," Berry says, "is not a gift. It needs

to be made, in response to nature. You can't talk about culture without talking about agriculture, because how your food is produced is cultural—the ultimate well-being. Our identity as human beings has to be conserved and you can't conserve your identity by yourself. You can't be generous or compassionate by yourself. You can't keep faith with anybody but God by yourself."

The phone rings. Somebody wants to know if Berry can help with the tobacco cutting.

Berry writes about care, thrift, the pleasures of rootedness, and good husbandry—in agriculture and in marriage. His values seem peculiar in a nation that so admires billionaires, movie stars, and sports heroes, a nation whose magazines and television shows are increasingly devoted to describing the lifestyles of the rich and famous. Berry's world is difficult, highly skilled, sweaty. In the tobacco patch, you'll never be a star.

I ask him, "How do you limit desire?"

"You can't. All of us desire heaven. But you must accept the limits. The things we've got to do is make things last. Suppose I mow that hillside in hot weather—I have to attend to the horses, their limits. If I exceed their limits, they'll die. I must obey their limits, the mower's limits, my limits. People think that limits are deadly dull, but knowing the limits is what makes elegance possible, and elegance is infinitely interesting."

He laughs. "If you get on that hillside with a team of horses, you won't need to ride the roller coaster." He pauses, looking out at the hillside he'd restored and the great, unpredictable river. "I don't think people know how interesting a little farm can be."

Wes

Jackson

The list of American prophets is quite short and few listed are white males. Sitting Bull, Chief Seattle, Black Elk, Joseph of the Nez Perce, Mother Jones, Martin Luther King, Henry David Thoreau. America's favored preachers have been revivalists, recalling us to dear childhood beliefs, refurbishing them, crying them with fresh passion, underlining them with the sweet harmonies of a gospel choir. I suppose there are some elderly Americans who remember the Reverend Billy Sunday. There may be some who even remember what he said.

Prophecy discomforts us. We—all of us—depend on the status quo for our daily bread, and poor people (the breadless, the homeless) wish nothing more than to join the status quo. Any tremor in the complex belief system we call American society might dislodge *us,* hurl *us* outside the gates.

Wes Jackson has described "the gift of denial," our ability to ignore what is patently obvious but too difficult or threatening to deal with. Prophecy is the flip side of the gift of denial. When

Jackson notes that we've built a civilization on fossil fuels that took sixty million years to lay down, fuels that will be exhausted in the next century, and that our civilization *must* change, cannot possibly continue as it is—that is prophecy. When he says that Africa's famine was partially caused by our kind willingness to cure those diseases that once killed most African infants, that is prophecy, too. Nobody said prophecy was going to be pleasant.

When he wonders if minds nurtured in a fossil fuel economy, with that economy's subtle presumptions, if those minds can even begin to imagine what society would be like without abundant cheap fuel, Jackson is at the limits of prophecy where reason falters and faith begins.

I nearly met Wes Jackson at a conference on sustainable agriculture. The ag school—I'll call it State Tech—had loaned their glossy conference center, with its elaborate dining facility, meeting rooms, and plush auditorium, but State Tech's agriculture professors showed their great enthusiasm for alternative farm practices by staying away. The audience was gray-haired ex-hippies, gentle bearded vegetarians and their wispy girlfriends, a half-dozen harried organic farmers and orchardists, a couple of sociologists researching the decline of rural America, and three concerned preachers. Wes Jackson, from the Land Institute, was guest speaker.

For balance, they'd invited an agribusiness spokesman, young Bill Owens, a tobacco and soybean farmer from the southern part of the state. Bill had been an honors graduate in agriculture from State Tech and was one of the Farm Bureau's young thrusters, "Farmer of the Year," volunteer spokesman for the status quo.

There were other speakers, too—a congressman's staffer and an international food expert delivered safe, inconsequential talks that give me a chance to find the men's room and browse through the photographic exhibit in the hall.

The young Bill Owens made his pitch, claiming that American agriculture was envied by the world, that one farmer feeds sixty-seven of us, that chemicals were unfortunately necessary—you know, *that* speech.

Journalists often describe Wes Jackson as outsized. "Isaiah crossed with a bison," "Broddingnagian." Wes is "ham-handed," "thick-fisted." But Jackson's hands are ordinary working hands and he isn't awfully big. He just *seems* big. Seated beside Bill Owens on the speakers' platform, Wes Jackson fidgeted: uncrossed and recrossed his legs, rocked back, hands locked behind his head, rocked forward to jot a note. Maybe his suit was too tight.

When Wes Jackson's turn came, he described a failed, inefficient agriculture; an agriculture that consumed more calories in fossil fuels than it produced in food; an agriculture that drained irreplaceable aquifers and polluted free-flowing streams. He spoke of a system that shattered rural communities to produce low-quality, sometimes dangerous, food. He warned of the danger to our culture, a culture with too many things "that once possessed cannot be done without." Jackson quoted from the ancient Greeks, the Bible. He quoted Mahatma Ghandi: "The world is big enough for all men's needs. It is not big enough for *one* man's greed."

Bill Owens floundered. "Maybe we don't like it, but we got to do it this way, Wes." (Bill hoped for an easy consensus.) "Maybe Wes wouldn't agree with me, but we got more in common than he thinks. I'll try those new plants he's growing out in Kansas." He turned. "How much you want for them seeds, Wes, and what kind of yield you get? We American farmers got to feed the world."

"That's not true," Wes Jackson snapped. "That's one of the falsehoods of American agriculture—'We have to feed the world.' We do not. Hungry people can't afford the food we produce. Over the long run people have to feed themselves. It is shameful to hope to take profit from others' starvation."

I felt sorry for Bill Owens, who, after all, was only repeating the foolishness he'd been taught. I thought Wes Jackson was scary, an unflinching man.

At the close, a folksinger sang Woodie Guthrie's "This Land Is Your Land," including the rarely sung verses denouncing private property. By the time I got up the nerve to introduce myself to Jackson, he'd split.

Salina, Kansas, is a short commuter hop from Kansas City near the Missouri. There are low hills, some with trees, but before long, the land gets very big and very flat. The Homestead Act broke this country into six-hundred-forty-acre sections, four one-hundred-sixty acre homesteads to a section, and dusty county roads box each section. It had been a dry year in Kansas; sandbars poked pale heads out of the riverbeds. Trees rumpled their banks, making the rivers seem like lengths of green gut squiggling across a chessboard. The tilled fields were big—eighty, ninety acres—and in the sunset the black soil looked almost purple.

Wes Jackson was easier here, home in Kansas, wearing blue jeans and a farmer's shirt. "You don't mind if we drop in at a meeting before I run you to your motel?" he asked.

Salina is a midsized Kansas town, supported by a Beechcraft plant, Exide Batteries, and agriculture. It has a couple of heartland motels, a Heartland Chevrolet, heartland this and that. Kansas doesn't think of itself as "the Midwest." It thinks of itself as "the heartland." That's an important distinction.

The meeting was held in the Hispanic part of town, eight sharp, in the Carver Community Center, where sixty people were organizing to fight a proposed lead smelter in Salina. When we took seats in the back, Dana Jackson was at the podium. She's an attractive woman with an easy smile. It became clear, as the meeting progressed, that lead smelter faced formidable, well-organized opponents. As each speaker came to the podium, he first gave his credentials as a Kansan. Wes leaned over to whisper capsule descriptions of his neighbors in the crowd. When one speaker detailed the ravages of lead poisoning, Wes folded his arms across his chest and murmured, "The bills of the Industrial Revolution are coming due." Suddenly he raised his hand and waggled it. "Say, all of you here opposed to this lead smelter," he drawled, "how many of you drive a car? How many of you drive a car with a *battery* in it?"

Everybody laughed. Somebody cried, "Will the sergeant at arms please remove that man?" Wes grinned too, but he was restless as a kid, couldn't sit still. "Let's get you to your motel."

Russell's is the kind of restaurant that could not exist outside of the heartland. Open twenty-four hours, no beer, a family place with a long, long menu, plenty of daily specials, and everything homemade and priced fair. Next morning, as Wes and I ate breakfast, a cook was complaining about baking thirty-six dozen cinnamon rolls for the night shift at Beechcraft. "To go," he moaned. Like all Russell's cooks, he was skinny, ill-shaven, and wore a farmer's grubby gimme cap: JOHN DEERE.

Wes Jackson and Dana are native Kansans. Wes grew up on a small farm and Dana's grandparents were early settlers. Wes told me about the struggle between pro- and anti-slavery forces before the Civil War. Although outnumbered four to one, the Kansas anti-slave forces did hold their own. "They were settlers," Wes explained. En route to a meeting, one of Dana's great-uncles was ambushed, shot at, and lost a bit of a piece of his ear. Uncle was a very religious man, but when he slid off his horse at the meeting house, he was in a fury. Hand clasped to his bloody ear, he exhorted his fellow settlers to pursue the ambushers. "Let us send them to he . . . to he . . . send them to THAT PLACE WHERE THE WICKED CUSTOMARILY CONGREGATE!"

Wes grins. He loves a good story.

Wes and Dana married in college and Wes took a good job (tenured) at Sacramento State University, doing genetic studies.

Dr. Jackson was on the fast track. But the Jacksons found that "California just wasn't the place to be," and they moved back to Kansas onto a twenty-eight-acre homestead overlooking the Little Smokey River. After a couple of years of figuring, puzzling, dreaming, they began the Land Institute. Wes was a natural teacher, it's in his bones. The Land Institute would be his school.

And, shortly, the Land Institute found its work, a grand, extraordinarily difficult task: to provide an alternative to conventional agriculture. Their alternative would be modeled on the absorptive, drought-resistant, noneroding, fecund Kansas prairie.

> Nature is at once uncompromising and forgiving, but we do not precisely know the degree of her compromise nor the extent of her forgiveness. I frankly doubt that we ever will. But we can say with a rather high degree of certainty that if we are to heal the split (between man and nature), it is the human agricultural system which must grow more toward the ways of nature rather than the other way around.
> —*New Roots for Agriculture*

As the Land Institute taught and designed genetic experiments on thousands of prairie legumes and grasses, Wes found time to write two books. The first was *New Roots for Agriculture,* and it established him as one of the most powerful agricultural critics alive. The second, *Altars of Unhewn Stone,* confirmed his early promise.

Running between steep bluffs, the Little Smokey River seems milky and low. I make some remark about how silted up it looks and Jackson is surprised. "Man, today, that's clear as a mountain stream."

Not like Virginia mountain streams, I say.

He asks if I'll talk to the students at their morning meeting.

It's a pleasant informal group. One young man worked for Catholic Charities in Africa, a woman is a recent botany graduate, another young man came from a Midwestern commercial farm. I described going back to the land in 1971, how startlingly ignorant we were. "Local trucks would go by our place real slow, and sometimes they'd go by real slow two or three times. We should have charged entertainment tax."

"How much of your living comes from your farm?"

"A third of our cash, almost all our food."

I said it was more difficult farming in an area where farming was going out. We have to buy every bit of our own equipment; we can't share or borrow or rent or get custom work done.

Afterward, Wes took me on a grand tour, beginning at the original twenty-eight acres. Clearly he enjoyed talking about the Institute's handmade beginnings, bridge planks sawn to build a barn, the used grain bins they used to dry their seeds. But the Institute has outgrown its spartan beginnings.

When the last of the Jacksons' kids left home, they sold the milk cow. No more chickens scratching around. The farm they bought next door had a modern ranch house on it, and that's Land Institute headquarters now. Wes grumbles about the Institute's new management team. He mutters, "The next time they ask me to fix the pump, I'll say, 'Get the management team to do it.'"

On the walls of Wes's office are detailed soil maps of Kansas and one of those joke "Licenses to Preach" signed by Dana. "Do you want a drink of water?" he asks. "It isn't very good." He's right.

There is nothing new about soil erosion. Plato complained about eroding hillsides in ancient Greece. Since 1935, the U.S. government has spent twenty billion dollars to combat erosion, but Wes notes, "Annual soil loss is greater now by at least twenty-five percent than in the Dust Bowl years when the SCS [Soil Conservation Service] was begun."

Picture Corsica, or the barren Greek hillsides, or desert Ethiopia. Now superimpose those parched pictures over Iowa and Kansas and Indiana and try to imagine what kind of American culture would flourish. There, that's prophecy.

Right across the road from the Land Institute office is a stretch of native prairie, never broken by a plow—natural prairie that serves as Jackson's check and inspiration. The grass was shorter than I'd expected, just knee-high, and I asked Wes about that; how about those pioneer accounts of big bluestem taller than a horse? "In the bottoms, where the ground is rich, sure, blue-stem'd come over a horse's withers." It was clumsy walking, through the matted, tangled grass which arrived in Kansas when the glaciers receded. I knelt and dug through to the soil, fine sandy loam, sweet to the tongue. They'd never need lime. In winter this country might get down to minus twenty; summers could soar above a hundred and ten. That's a pretty extreme range. "How much is land per acre?" I asked.

"Two hundred fifty to four hundred an acre. Depends how close to town." Wes said tiny rural Kansas towns were drying up; you could buy a small house (city water and sewer) in prairie towns west of here for three thousand dollars.

Recently, with great hoopla, some of the land-grant ag schools celebrated their hundredth year of service to agriculture: a hundred years of presiding over the demise of their clients. Impoverished rural communities, fewer and fewer farmers on more and more acres, their steady migration to the cities seen as inevitable, part of a process beyond our decisions, something sad but true.

But our values determined that exodus, our belief that farm work was helpless drudgery, that it was always the "marginal" (read "shiftless") farmers who failed. "Marginal" seems a category reserved for farmers. We never hear of "marginal" congressmen or "marginal" government economists.

Dwight Eisenhower grew up on a Kansas farm and was Dana's distant kin. Wes Jackson sighed. "We lost a good one when we lost him. What a farmer he would have made."

In agriculture, as in all cultures, values direct our inquiries. When Monsanto instructs its seed division to breed (or gene splice) for a corn variety that is resistant to Monsanto herbicides, they are valuing an industrial, chemical agriculture powered by fossil fuels and debt.

> How we look at the world is how it becomes. I believe, for example, that there is a law of human ecology that, bluntly stated, is: "Values dictate genotype." I think we can safely say that our major crops, for example, corn, soybeans, and wheat, have genes that we might call "Chicago Board of Trade Genes." There are also wellhead genes and computer genes. In other words, there are ensembles of genes in our major crops that would not exist in their particular constellation were there not a Chicago Board of Trade . . . or fossil fuel wellheads or computers. Our values arrange even the molecules of heredity.
>
> —*Altars of Unhewn Stone*

Besides native prairie, the Land Institute's 225 acres is in experimental plots where Jackson breeds and selects from species —prairie perennials—nobody has ever (consciously) bred from before.

What they seek is a high-yielding perennial polyculture to replace annuals like corn, soybeans, and wheat. At minimum, they hope to create new feed grains or excellent forage. At best, they dream of perennial edible grains ("Another slice of bundleflower bread, dear? More of that nice leymus soup?").

When *Country Journal* first wrote about the Land Institute ("Taking on the Agricultural Establishment," July 1983), Jackson was searching the world for genetic materials. Four thousand odd species later, he's narrowed the candidates: eastern gamma grass, leymus (a Siberian wild rye), Illinois bundleflower, a potentially perennial grain sorghum and (perhaps) a sunflower variety. Presently he's concentrating on seed yield (it's the seeds we eat, after all) and shatter resistance (if a seed head breaks up as soon as seeds are ripe, it can't be harvested effectively). His plots test interdependency, water absorption, resistance to plant pathogens. Edibility is a few years (fifty? one hundred?) down the road.

When Jackson first announced his plans, back in 1974, traditional plant geneticists thought he had a screw loose. To survive on the prairie—it had been thought—plants either develop strong roots *or* numerous seeds. Man's cultivated annuals come from the seed bearers; the strong-rooted erosion-proof perennials produce few not-vigorous seeds. Getting a successful stand of bluestem from seed is fairly difficult.

Most geneticists thought Jackson's high-yielding perennial polyculture was an idea on a par with perpetual-motion machines. Now they're not so sure. Several "respectable" universities have drawn from Jackson's experiments.

After a day of hiking the plots and talking, Jackson showed me into a small tenant house on the most recently acquired patch of Land Institute land. Here they provided fresh organic vegetable to Salina all summer, across the road from the proposed lead smelter. Jackson said the water here was much better. It was. It came, he said, from a different part of the Salina aquifer.

Wes Jackson grew up Methodist and sometimes teaches at the local Sunday School. He believes that an individual should work out his religious life within his own culture: in America, Christianity. When Gary Snyder wrote Ed Abbey congratulating him on a new book, Abbey wrote back. "Yeah, I like your poetry too. Except for all that Bhuddist crap." Wes grinned. "Ed was like a teenager. You never could trap him."

> Christ's metaphors are biological or cultural. He spoke of the vine and the branches, of fish and fishermen. . . . The Christian message, like an ecosystem, is about process. In an ecological sense, the cross symbolizes a willingness to die so that the continuation of life might be served.
> —*Altars of Unhewn Stone*

Jackson calls the change from a hunter-gatherer society to till agriculture "the fall," and clearly the native prairie is his Eden.

But Jackson is no revivalist. He quotes, "Religions are codifications of energy transfer," and that's how he describes the Amish failure on the Great Plains. Bound as they were to draft animals for traction, they failed to prosper in the dry, big landscape. Some turned to tractors, others returned to a region with more rainfall. "Draft animals prevented Amish spread," Jackson tells me. "The codification of their religious ethic restricted them."

Earlier that afternoon, on the edge of the newly purchased land, Jackson pointed to a road, hidden in a brushy fencerow. At first I couldn't identify it as a road, it was so badly sited and overgrown. One consequence of six-hundred-forty-acre sections broken into one-hundred-sixty-acre homesteads was that each homestead had road access. Later, as heirs broke up their homesteads, the inside forty acres of each homestead was landlocked. Usually the right-of-way followed a fence line, dead straight, oblivious to erosion potential. Jackson shook his head. "If this country had been settled by a more homogeneous people, they might have put that road where it'd do less harm. That is the practical consequence of not loving your neighbor as yourself."

Jackson thinks farm programs that give money directly to farmers are mistaken, that farmers simply pass their money to equipment and chemical manufacturers. He would like to see programs that support the rural infrastructure.

I told him about a neighbor of mine, a first-rate mechanic and welder who had to take a job in town. For him, a two-hour daily commute for seven dollars an hour. For us farmers, nobody to help when the hay balers broke down in the field and rain threatening. Either we could abandon the hay and haul the baler into town or beg the equipment dealer to dispatch his repair truck, over the mountain, for only one customer when dozens of nearer farmers were clamoring for it.

"That's where the government money should go," Jackson said. "We should subsidize that welder."

On the way back to my motel, Jackson pointed at a brand-new shopping center under construction, just slightly nearer to the highway than the old one, which would be torn down. Tax advantages, easier shopping, more fertile land gone.

I said, "Wendell Berry once wrote that soil is an ultimate value. Can you think of any other ultimate values?"

He was silent for a moment. "Well, there's water...."

"Oh, sure, Wes, and air, and—"

"The Kingdom of God," Wes Jackson said.

Maury

Telleen

W hen they find out how much money we make on the
farm, our city friends shake their heads. "Why
bother? Why not sell out and move back to town? It's
so *remote* out here."

I suppose we could. We could probably get enough for our
two-hundred-eighty-acre farm to buy a house and lot in the Washington, D.C. suburbs—one of those places real-estate agents call
"starter houses." Or we could find a two-bedroom apartment in
New York City (a one-bedroom in a better neighborhood).

We'd auction off the farm machinery, the hay equipment,
the 1951 Dodge Power Wagon, the tools. In the city we wouldn't
need the Allen wrenches, the post hole digger, or the pipe dies.
We could sell the air compressor, the cutting torch, the fence
stretcher, the bolt buckets. It would be a relief to get rid of all that
junk.

If we were to move, I suppose I'd miss the quiet. Cities buzz

...kle all the time. But it would be nice to live where we could order Chinese. I'd be curious to see MTV.

But in thinking about leaving here, I get only so far before running into a bedrock problem: What would we do with the animals? We have a hundred and twenty ewes, six rams, ten barn cats, and four border collies. It's taken fifteen years to build that flock. They're fall lambers, good mothers, and they lamb without aid. One of our dogs is old; another, deaf. If we left, I'd have to put them down.

Who would put food out for the barn cats? And what would *our* life be like? So much of what we do has to do with the animals. Remember the time our bitch Lucille got bit by a copperhead? The time Granma, the aged ewe, gave birth by Caesarean section? The day the hogs got under the house?

I wonder if we haven't come to depend on the animals as much as they depend on us. So I decided to talk about that with Maury Telleen, Editor of *The Draft Horse Journal*. He understands one's relationship to the land. And nobody knows more about farm animals than Maury.

> If you are thinking of draft horses in terms of "a return to the simple life," I think you had better reexamine your motives. There is nothing simple or simple-minded about farming with horses. I think it safe to say that any man who can ...do a good job of plowing with four or five horses on a two-bottom gang can, with but a few hours' instruction and practice, do the same with a tractor. The reverse can no way apply.... It is more difficult to make a candle than to flip a switch.
> —Maury Telleen, *The Draft Horse Primer*

Waverly, Iowa, is on the edge of the state's mixed farmland. Farther west they grow corn and soybeans, and the farmers who can afford it fly south for the winter. Waverly isn't far from the Minnesota line and was settled by German and Scandinavian Lutherans. Your waitress brings coffee as soon as you sit down and keeps pouring throughout the meal. Black coffee. Cream and sugar are a little effete.

Out the window and across the road, a tremendous double-tired John Deere is wallowing across the field. According to the local paper, sixty percent of the corn has been planted. It's been droughty here for three years and farmers are anxious about rain. It's supposed to rain, but today, May 9, over the rumpled hills of eastern Iowa, the great sky sparkles blue. The paper notes that farm foreclosures are down from the mid-1980s, but bankers will be sending out a few foreclosure notices this month. Here, as in the rest of America, good farmers are still going under.

Waverly's economy depends on Wartburg College, Carnation (instant breakfast), Century Insurance, and Koehlring (makers of cranes and heavy equipment). Traditionally the towns out here depended on agriculture, but that's less true today, and the rural farm populace is in steady decline.

> Our little towns are under a lot of stress. Some, in the areas west and south of here, have less population than they've had since the Civil War. Kids have to travel 40 or 50 miles each day to school. The *Des Moines Register* calls it "The Dakota-ization of Iowa."
>
> —Maury Telleen

The Draft Horse Journal is located in new offices on the outskirts of Waverly, sharing a building with the Waverly Mental Health Clinic, a fact Maury enjoys quite a bit. The *Journal*'s office is like any other: coffee machine, long tables for laying out pages, heaps of the old agricultural journals Maury buys at farm sales.

There's a nineteenth-century framed lithograph of The Holbert Horse Company of Greely, Iowa. It shows the horse barns, sales barns, and grooms holding several hundred horses. "Old A. B. Holbert thought the business was going to go on forever," Maury tells me. "He sent his sons to be educated in Europe so they could speak the exporter's language." He points at the horse barns. "All those buildings are gone now."

In 1918 there were twenty million horses in America. Draft horses—the big Percherons, Clydesdales, Belgians, Suffolks, and Shires—occupied the center ring at all the livestock shows and expositions. To the astonished delight of the heavy-horse breeders, a Belgian stallion, Farceur, brought $47,500 at auction. Maury has written about this time when "the draft horse breeders of America were about as optimistic as they would ever get. They had a few more gravy train years ahead, but not many."

The tractor replaced their animals. The state agricultural schools dispersed their breeding stock, draft horses were kicked out of the big state fairs (they weren't modern enough), and by 1950 so few horses were left in the United States that the USDA census stopped counting them.

Maury Telleen is a short man ("sixteen hands high") who makes small decisions quickly. He's hard to keep up with. He and his wife, Jeannine, grew up on Iowa farms where horses were still worked. His father used to show Brown Swiss cattle. For a while Maury worked out west before coming back to Iowa in 1956 to manage the Waterloo Cattle Congress. Between shows he grazed his sheep on the grassy parking lots. He used horses to haul manure from the show barns, to mow, and to hitch up for hayrides.

He suggested to the Clydesdale directors at the cattle congress that they should have a sale. Sale announcements went out, and after a while the entries came back—two of them. The directors wanted to cancel the sale.

"So long as we get ten or fifteen people bidding," Maury argued, "we can have a sale." They went ahead and sold the two Clydesdales, and it was a good sale. But, Maury grins, "It *was* brief." Last year, in Springfield, Illinois, the National Clydesdale Sale sold a hundred eleven horses.

In 1964, Maury and Jeannine decided to start *The Draft Horse*

Journal. On their kitchen table they hand-assembled and addressed the fifteen hundred copies of their first issue. They thought it would be a part-time enterprise, but today the *Journal* has twenty-four thousand subscribers and a staff of five.

Most American farm magazines are awful. They bow to their big advertisers, keep mum about the excesses of agribusiness, and if they have an editorial policy at all, it's to cuss the animal-rights people, cuss the environmentalists, and cuss the government (unless a farm handout is threatened). Some of these magazines will sell their front cover for an ad.

The *Journal* comes from an older tradition. In his cluttered office, Maury keeps his collections of venerable (now defunct) agricultural publications such as *The Breeder's Gazette, The American Breeder,* and *Wallace's Farmer.*

Leafing through these dusty periodicals is an eye opener. They are more intelligent than our modern magazines and they assume their readers are intelligent, too. They had a grand purpose: to make strong farms and strong farm families. Maury says, "They made citizens."

You can't buy the *Journal*'s mailing list of subscribers. You can't even advertise unless you're selling something connected with draft horses. Maury publishes writers like Wendell Berry and Gene Logsdon, and his editorials are blunt and surprising.

> I don't wish to see us create a new priesthood of doomsday ecologists and philosophers, for all priesthoods are suspect. But they have a lot of evidence on their side.... It is time they had at least "equal time" with the people who sell hamburgers and shoes and magazines and weapons and elections.
>
> Which brings us to restraint. I think that may be the hardest thing of all. To get over the notion that we are "in charge."
>
> So here is what I think we ought to do ... while we are thinking about all these things. I think we should all plant some trees. It will help a little bit.
> —Editorial, *The Draft Horse Journal,* Summer 1989

The first trees Maury planted, in a long row between his upper fields, were silver maple, but they didn't do well in the sandy soil. So he replanted with ash. The Telleen farm is sixty hilly acres. "Twenty-five percent of the class-one soil in the world is in Iowa," Maury jokes. "And I don't have a shovelful of it." He strides through the fields at a pretty good clip. Over there is alfalfa. He'll take a cutting of it before he plows it down for corn. His oats are up; bird's-foot trefoil is just flowering. The alfalfa in his top field was burned out by the drought. He thinks he'll plant Sudan grass there next time.

This is a small, working farm, not an estate. The outbuildings are more practical than picturesque, with a flock of Oxford ewes in old cinder-block hog housing. On these sixty acres Maury raises almost all the feed he needs for fifty sheep and a half-dozen horses.

Although I know he shows his sheep at The National Oxford Show, and brings horses to some of the draft horse shows, I don't see any trophies—until he opens a closet in the house to show me his show harness. The harness is immaculately kept. The rows of trophies on the floor are gathering dust.

He is, however, awfully proud of his week-old Percheron foal, a spindle-legged, stout-bodied filly who weighs two hundred pounds already. Her coat is fuzzy, like a puppy's. Maury scratches the foal from the top of her tail to the nape of her neck. "I never knew a foal who didn't like this," he said, grinning.

Maury and his hired man talk about the mare they bred last weekend to a young, inexperienced stallion. They are both pleased that the mating went well and that neither mare nor stallion got hurt. Tomorrow, if it isn't too wet, he'll take the horses out and let me drive the team.

You should understand that heavy horses are just that—some weigh more than a ton. I'm six feet one and I can barely see over their withers. I tell Maury I am totally ignorant of horses: "Incompetent," I blurt.

"We'll settle for 'ignorant,' " Maury says dryly.

The next morning at breakfast Maury shows me an Allis-Chalmers tractor ad from decades ago that shows a farm family sitting on the porch, the men smoking their pipes, while in the next field a neighboring horse farmer is still trying to get his work done. Maury thinks the tractor makers were innocents. "Their assumption was that people could change their means of power without changing the common lifestyle." He tapped the ad. "They never dreamed their new tractor would replace that neighbor. And three others as well."

There is never one cause of a major cultural change, and real heroes and villains are rare. The companies that made the tractors also manufactured horse-drawn implements. If they failed to dedicate many research dollars to the horse implements, who could blame them?

Unlike the neighbor who wanted cash when he sold you a horse, tractor dealers offered credit. The ag schools and government agencies were fascinated by the tractor, and there was peer pressure among farmers to buy one.

So they killed all those horses. You may recall supermarket shelves in the late 1940s and 1950s, row on row of cheap, canned horsemeat for dogs. "State fair and international champions were sent to the kill," Maury says. "The gene pools shrank. Some [purebred horse] families survived in the hands of people who could afford to ignore the market, but some of the best families also got killed. It's kind of a wonder the blooming horses came through in the shape they did."

The effect of the shift to tractors was enormous. In a horse-drawn agriculture, men farmed what they could see, what they and their families could handle. The big new machines enabled fewer and fewer farmers to produce crops on more and more land; production, for its own sake, became the only goal. Forget conservation of land, of families, of communities—bushels per acre was what mattered. And, of course, despite the innocent hopes of that early Allis-Chalmers ad, tractors didn't bring the farmer more free time. After he bought his neighbor's land, he had to plow all night to pay for it. You can't plow at night with horses.

Jeannine brings out a platter of bacon and eggs and pours more coffee. One of the Telleen children is an architect, another a horseman at the Budweiser stables, still another a wildlife biologist. The youngest is a veterinarian. All the kids grew up experiencing the joys and heartbreaks of animals.

Maury talks about those cattle breeders who keep a few head of cattle just for the shows. "Their animals are possessions. They might as well have a big boat parked up there. I see cattle, sheep, and horses as part of an integrated farm enterprise. I don't think I'm a horse lover. If there was nothing for a draft horse to do in my life, I wouldn't want to own him."

Maury pushes his plate back and asks if I'm ready to drive a team.

"I guess so," I say.

It's a bit above freezing when we go out to the horse barn, and I'm glad of the sweater under my jacket. "Here," Maury says, "you harness her."

The harness is heavy and awkward, but I manage to flop the rig over the beast's back. Quickly, precisely, Maury runs me through the harnessing. "Seat the hames, hook the breast strap into the lower hame ring—this is where she pulls, from the point —hook the bellyband." He tells the horse to move over. She does. Her name is Rose. She is fourteen years old.

Often draft horses are called gentle giants, but Maury doesn't like the phrase. "That puts draft horses in the light of panda bears. They are big, athletic animals, and if you're careless or ignorant, you can get hurt." I feel ignorant.

Rose is black. March, her harness mate, is a dapple-gray, heavy in foal. The two beasts set off down the hill, towing Maury like a chip behind them. "Walk," he says, and, by God, that's what they do.

"These horses are a little better broke than most, because they get more work than most," he says.

In his equipment shed, Maury keeps his horse-drawn mower, cultipacker, harrow, planter, seeder, and the forecart (the "Amish tractor") horse farmers use when they convert tractor machinery to horse-drawn. He loads bales of hay into the manure spreader so I can ride comfortably. "My horses don't hate to pull. My horses like to work. And I don't think that's a rationalization." He clucks the beasts through the first gate and halfway up the hill before he asks me to give it a go.

The lines are as thick as a man's leather belt, stiff and cold. Although the horses are well gaited, the ride isn't machine-smooth. We proceed at a clip-clop pace. I perch on the high steel seat with only the lines between me and two enormous horses. Fortunately, the animals seem to know their business.

Maury gives me occasional instructions. "Every beginner tries to make the horse turn by sticking his arm out. The horse can't see your arm. Watch your elbows. Let the lines slip through."

I drive the horses around and around in a small field. They steer delicately and precisely. I have more control than I do on my tractor. It begins to sleet, and the frozen granules bounce off my jacket and hands. Maury offers me his gloves but I say no.

Draft horses have tremendous hooves that don't leave much of a mark (flotation, it's called), even on ground so soft it would bog my tractor in an instant.

"Stop the horses. Make them back."

"Back," I say, conversationally. They do. "Walk," I say. They don't budge. Maury says "Walk" is a slow-down command, not a start command. "Get up," I say and they do.

All the best agricultures are regional, tied to the requirements of a specific place, soil, climate, and people. Regional agriculture is why we have so many breeds of domestic animals. "Cheap transportation has been the curse of good regional agriculture," Maury says. "Cheap petroleum has been hard on the gene pool, and when it's no longer cheap and we have to become regionally self-sufficient, we've going to miss some of these breeds. Cheap petroleum has subsidized too-rapid change at an artificially low price."

Maury Telleen doesn't seek a return to the horse farming of the past. He does think that the horse can be a practical addition to the small family farm. Horses eat farm-grown feed, return fertility to the soil, produce their own replacements, and work when tractors must stay in the machine shed. They promote small farms and a desirable human culture.

In America, where so much agriculture is in disarray, a sound model can be found in the Amish. Their farms are productive, their communities stable, their families more content than most. And the structure of Amish farming is based on the horse. More and more farmers on the outskirts of Amish communities are turning to horses for some farmwork, in part because the Amish infrastructure provides harness makers and horse sense. And, on small tracts, horses are particularly useful for logging and bringing in firewood. They do so much less damage in the woods than giant skidders do.

Many modern farmers see horses as mere nostalgia. Maury sees them as part of a productive future.

I turn Rose and March downhill through the narrow gate. I stop. I back. There's a tremendous sense of power when you're sitting behind all that brute muscle.

I can't be enthusiastic about the direction we are going. There is so much land amassed in the hands of so few. That's why we fled Europe a hundred years ago. When farms get big enough, really careless things happen.

I don't think anybody cares so long as food is plentiful and food is cheap and *I* don't have to work all those hours. Americans hold manual labor in contempt. I fear for a nation too proud to weed its own garden.

—Maury Telleen

Back in the barn, the horses steam. The harness was clumsy going on and now it's clumsy coming off. "If you don't hang it up right, the next man will curse you." I hang it up right.

A sound, broke draft horse will fetch a thousand dollars at one of the big auctions. Fancier models go higher, and horses suitable for the brewery hitches can bring spectacular prices. New harness costs about eight hundred dollars. For beginners there are horsemanship schools.

We're not quite finished with my lesson. Maury leads the week-old foal out into the paddock and her mother follows. The best time to start working with a foal is when she's small, and already Maury is putting the youngster on a lead. For a couple of days he will use a clothesline around the filly's rump to keep her coming forward.

The filly is worried—she jumps and bucks—but her ancestors have been bred for centuries to work with man, originally as war horses and later in the fields. Handled properly, this Percheron filly will more than earn her feed one day.

Maury says, "Here. You take her."

So I take the lead and walk backward around the filly's mother. The youngster more or less follows. I have a live thing on the end of the rope and can feel her brain, muscles, and character.

Earlier today, Maury spoke about the relationship between men and animals. "Everybody needs to be terribly important to someone or something."

Now he says, "That's a dandy colt."

I think so too, leading her around her mother, just at the start of her brilliant career.

Acknowledgments

Grateful acknowledgment is made to: *The Atlantic, Country Journal, Dog Fancy, GQ, Harper's,* and National Public Radio's "All Things Considered," where some of these pieces first appeared, and to The Virginia Historical Society for permission to reprint letters from Isaac Gwin and Elizabeth Gum.

Hugh McAden's journal was first cited in William Henry Foote's *Sketches of North Carolina* (1846), the Wilson family memoir was originally published in the *Kanawha Gazette* in 1887, and the account of the aftermath of Braddock's defeat is from Francis Parkman's *France and England in North America* (1956).

I would not have found my way through the thicket of history without the help of Dr. Ken Koons, Mrs. Ann (McClintlock) Lockridge, Mr. Randy Richardson, Miss Marie Stuart, and Mrs. Helen (Stuart) Knecht. Thank you. Where I went wrong is my doing, not yours.

And special thanks to my neighbors, who have entrusted me with their stories to tell.

The author and the publisher wish to thank the photographers for permission to reprint the following: The farm, page 50, by Jeane Bice; A.E. Stephenson, neighbor, page 51, and country store with Randolph Hodge and Nelson Wright, page 131, by Cynthia Johnson; Anne McCaig and newborn lamb, page 94, by Ethan Sprague; Gael in the tub, page 95, by Joel Richardson, courtesy of the Washington Post Company, Inc.